Gluten-free
Cookbook

contents

food for thought 4

breakfast 10

the lunchbox 22

kids' parties 42

baking 64

glossary 122

conversion chart 125

index 126

food for thought

If you have an allergy or food sensitivity in the family, the thought of living without warm crusty bread, mouth-watering muffins, and scrumptious cakes can be devastating.

Certainly in decades past, allergy-free baking has not been everyone's cup of carrot juice. Just the mention of "gluten-free" conjured up images of cakes that felt like stone and tasted like cardboard.

We could only lament those poor, allergy-prone children, eating odd, uninspiring meals in the far corner of the playground, or being tragically ushered away from the birthday cake.

And pity the poor mothers who spent their lives peering, probing, and poring over every morsel of food within an inch of its life – all in case a trace of nut may be lurking.

The bad news is that allergies may only get worse with global warming as hotter, drier conditions set up our bodies for heightened immune reactions.

It's possible, too, that some behavioral problems in children may be linked to diet, particularly sensitivity to food chemicals and gluten.

For the modern mom and dad, this means rather than a food allergy being a rare occurrence, you can expect at least two or three of the children you invite to your child's birthday party to have some sort of food sensitivity or allergy.

The good news is there's plenty you can do about it, and whether you're cooking for allergies in your own family or simply have the social smarts and good conscience to make a gluten-free birthday cake for your child's friends, we've covered all bases with the recipes in this book.

what is Celiac Disease?

Despite a common misconception, Celiac Disease is not actually an allergy, but rather an auto-immune disease that causes damage to the lining of the small intestine when gluten is consumed. Just as people with nut allergies avoid nuts, the only way to treat Celiac Disease is to avoid wheat, rye, barley, and oat products. Celiac Disease is diagnosed by a blood screening test (tissue transglutaminase) that your doctor can arrange, followed by a small-bowel biopsy by a gastroenterologist for confirmation. Celiac Disease should not be confused with wheat allergy, which rarely occurs beyond infancy, or the stomach and bowel irritation that gluten can sometimes cause in people with chemical intolerances, who may also benefit from a gluten-free diet.

There is much variability in the severity of Celiac Disease with relatively mild to quite severe symptoms listed below. If you have Celiac

Disease, it's not a case of a little gluten every now and then won't hurt. It's essential that you maintain a strict gluten-free diet. While some foods like wheat, rye, and barley have to be strictly avoided, other foods such as pure, uncontaminated oats are tolerated by some people with Celiac Disease, but not by others – to be on the safe side, oats are best avoided completely. To take the agony out of your shopping, we have provided a list of foods that are safe to eat for anyone on a gluten-free diet. While this list is not complete, it certainly gives you a good indication of foods that should be avoided.

spotting the symptoms of Celiac Disease

The symptoms of Celiac Disease include fatigue, lack of energy, low iron levels, unusual or excessive wind or burping, feeling full after only a small amount of food, bloating, stomach cramps, diarrhea, poor weight gain or delayed growth, or sometimes weight gain. Less common symptoms include bruising easily, mouth ulcers, depression, dental problems, miscarriages, and joint and bone problems. People with Celiac Disease tend to be more likely to be at risk of osteoporosis because of poor absorption of nutrients to the bones. Celiac Disease also tends to be a multi-system disorder and can often go hand-in-hand with other auto-immune diseases, especially type 1 Diabetes, thyroid problems, and a severe skin condition called Dermatitis Herpitiformis.

the gluten-free diet

Living and eating with gluten intolerance or allergy doesn't have to be fussy or expensive, if you know a few shortcuts. Here are our top tips for gluten-free baking:

• Don't waste a flop just because you're cooking gluten-free. If your fruitcake or mud cake is a disaster, break it up, mix with a little alcohol and dip in melted chocolate for delicious truffles. Save all stale/unused bread for meatloaf, stuffing, casserole toppings, etc. If cookies fall apart, crumble them in layers with yogurt or make a trifle out of them. You can also use them as a base for a cheesecake.

• Be precise. Keep measuring cups for dry ingredients and also a measuring cup for wet. Being exact is an important rule for any baking, but even more so in gluten-free cooking as gluten is the very element in wheat flour that holds things together and gives baked goods their spring. In gluten-free cooking, there's a lot of chemical science involved as you are often using more than one flour, each of a different texture and consistency. Rice flour, for instance, is gritty, while soy flour is finer. The good news is that we've done the hard work for you in the Test Kitchen to work out exactly the right ratios. So measure precisely and use the flours prescribed rather than taking the "any old flour will do" approach. And always be sure to use a spatula to level off the top and flatten the surface to achieve the most accurate measurement with dry ingredients.

top tip

Read the label every time. Some foods that appear acceptable may contain gluten, but this will be declared on the product label. Manufacturers also regularly change ingredients. Remember, wheat-free doesn't always mean gluten-free as the product may still contain rye, barley, oats, or spelt. If you eat some gluten by accident, you may have stomach cramps or diarrhea or even no symptoms. But even small amounts of gluten can damage the intestines if you have Celiac Disease – it's not low-gluten, it's no gluten.

• Beware of some labels – not all foods are what they seem. Most cornflakes, for instance, contain malt extract (barley), while confectioner's sugar mixture may contain wheat. We use pure confectioner's sugar instead, which contains only sugar.

• Always cover gluten-free baked goods as they can dry out quickly.

• Find a gluten-free or allergy-free cooking buddy. Trying things is much more fun when you can find a kindred spirit.

• Store, label, and use gluten-free flours and non-gluten-free flours separately to avoid contamination.

• Pastry and biscuit dough is easier to handle if refrigerated.

• After baking cakes, breads, muffins, etc., wrap and freeze them. Wrapping items individually allows you to use just what is required.

• Oven temperature is important in the baking of gluten-free foods. If you are having ongoing problems with gluten-free baking, check your oven temperature. Oven thermometers can be purchased from a kitchenware shop.

what you can eat

If you have Celiac Disease or a gluten sensitivity these are the foods you can eat:

• All fresh fruit and vegetables.

• Dairy: milk, cream, cheese, most yogurts, butter, margarine, cottage cheese, sour cream, most ice creams (check labels for an ingredient from a gluten source, or cake or cookie bits). Corn syrup from wheat is gluten-free and okay even though it sounds like it isn't.

• Beef, pork, lamb, poultry, veal, fish and shellfish, eggs, dried beans, peas, tofu, plain nuts, and peanut butter.

- Check ingredients on all manufactured or pressed meats and all canned goods.
- Oils, butter, and margarine.
- Herbs and most spices (but check labels for wheat as an ingredient).
- All alcohol except beer (though gluten-free beers are now available).
- Plain rice cakes, rice crackers, popcorn, plain potato, and corn chips.
- Canned tuna, chicken, canned beans and lentils, some spaghetti sauces (check labels).
- Beverages like fruit juices, instant and ground coffee, tea, soft drinks.
- Check labels on all condiments such as mustard, ketchup, horseradish and jellies, relish, pickles, olives, and vanilla.
- Sugar, honey, salt and pepper.
- Rice and corn cereals without malt extract (barley), rice puffs, rice bran, buckwheat puffs, millet puffs, amaranth, sorghum, gluten-free granola, rice porridge, and psyllium husks.
- Gluten-free pasta, rice noodles, or vermicelli.
- Gluten-free stock and gravy are now available.

did you know?
Check labels when choosing candies – corn syrup made from wheat is actually gluten-free.

what you can't eat

If you have Celiac Disease or a gluten sensitivity, these are the foods you need to avoid:

- Wheat, barley, rye, farina, graham flour, semolina, durum, bulgur, kamut, kasha, matzo meal, spelt, triticale, malt (from barley), malt extract (from barley), and oats. While oats affect some people with Celiac Disease but not others, it is best avoided completely.
- Remember most processed foods from grains contain gluten. Avoid these foods unless they're labeled as gluten-free or made with corn, rice, soy, or other gluten-free grain. These foods include breads, cereals, crackers, croutons, pasta and cookies, cakes and pies.
- Check ingredients on other processed foods such as soups, gravies, sauces (including soy sauce), many candies, imitation meat or seafood, processed luncheon meats, self-basting poultry.
- Food additives such as thickeners and starches made from wheat.
- Medications and vitamins that use wheat starch as a binding agent.
- Playdough, made from wheat flour – young children often eat playdough when they play with it, so be alert if your child has Celiac Disease.

other food allergies

Food allergies differ from one person to the next. While for one person eating egg or drinking milk may cause bowel symptoms or skin rashes, those who are highly allergic may have a life-threatening reaction that can stop them breathing.

spotting the symptoms

The symptoms of food allergies can range from, most commonly, hives and eczema to, less commonly, low blood pressure, dizziness, or faintness. Swelling of the lips and throat, which in severe cases can cause difficulty breathing (anaphylaxis) is a rare, but life-threatening symptom. Other common food allergy signs include diarrhea, vomiting, dry, itchy throat and tongue, coughing, wheezing, and a runny or blocked nose.

top tip
If planning to dine at a restaurant, it is a good idea to phone in advance. This way you can learn what is on the menu, ask about ingredients, and explain what you cannot eat. If you are not confident about getting a gluten-free meal after speaking to the restaurant, it would be wise to go elsewhere.

what you can't eat

Foods that may be detrimental for people with egg, nut, and dairy allergies include the following:

- **egg:** For those who have an egg allergy remember to watch out for the presence of eggs in foods where labels mention albumin, egg solids, egg substitutes, eggnog, globulin, livetin, lysozyme, mayonnaise, meringue, ovalbumin, ovamucin, ovmucoid, ovovilen, and vitellen. Watch out for ice creams, custards, soups, and many decadent desserts like soufflé, tiramisu, and crème caramel.

- **nuts:** People with nut and seed allergies should always read labels for traces of nuts or sesame. Apart from the obvious, like peanut butter, nuts can also be in nougat or marzipan, chocolates and cakes, crackers, cereals, and other baked goods. Even some shampoos have traces of sesame seed, poppy seed, and cotton seed that can lead to itchiness or even severe reactions for some people. For people allergic to sesame, don't forget common culprits like hummus, stir-fries, and chutney. And, of course, tahini, bagels, bread sticks, and veggie burgers.

• **dairy:** And if it's dairy that you're allergic to or if you have lactose intolerance? Remember, cows' milk is not only found in butter, cream, milk, and cheese, among other dairy foods, but is also disguised on labels as whey, casein, hydrosalates (casein, milk protein, whey, and whey protein), caseinates (calcium, ammonium, magnesium, potassium, sodium). Other culprits are lactalbumin, lactoglobulin, lactose, and Opta (fat substitute). Speak to your doctor about other ways to get enough calcium in your diet.

menu tips

Home is covered, but what about dining out? Here are some hidden terms for gluten that you need to watch for:
• Au gratin – a topping of breadcrumbs and cheese.
• Béchamel – white sauce made by thickening milk with a butter and flour mixture.
• Cordon bleu – chicken or veal dish with ham and cheese that is crumbed (breadcrumbs) and fried.
• Encrusted – may use flour or breadcrumbs to bind ingredients.
• Dusted – sprinkled with flour.
• Farfel – a soup garnish made of minced noodle dough.
• Marinade – this may contain soy sauce.

Note: These lists are not exhaustive. For further advice consult your allergist.

food intolerances

Food intolerances are not the same as a food allergy. An intolerance means you may experience an adverse reaction to certain foods, but this does not involve the immune system.

You can also generally tolerate a little of these foods before you experience symptoms, such as stomach and bowel upsets, bloating, hives, and headaches. While the symptoms can be unpleasant, they are generally not life threatening. Comprehensive assessment by an allergist or immunologist can help determine the type of allergy or intolerance.

In The *Gluten-free Cookbook* we understand that you're committed to good health, a household budget, and fuss-free cooking.

Of the 50 mouth-watering recipes in this book, all are wheat-flour-free for gluten-sensitive folks, while others are specifically tailored for people with life-threatening nut allergies or those with the itchy and scratchy life that goes with an egg or dairy allergy. Just follow the key at the beginning of the recipe to ensure you're cooking for your allergy condition (gluten-free, wheat-free, yeast-free, dairy-free, egg-free, or nut-free). All ingredients are available in supermarkets, specialty foods shops, or health food stores.

breakfast

These five delicious recipes for both weekday and weekend breakfasts are a surprise and a delight. Who would have thought allergy-free food could taste so good?

waffles with maple syrup

This recipe is gluten-free, wheat-free, yeast-free, and dairy-free.

1 Beat spread, superfine sugar, and vanilla in medium bowl with electric mixer until light and fluffy. Beat in egg yolks, one at a time.
2 Beat egg whites in small bowl with electric mixer until soft peaks form, fold into egg-yolk mixture.
3 Fold in sifted dry ingredients and water. Do not overmix. (Mixture may look slightly curdled.)
4 Spray heated waffle iron with cooking oil; pour ½-cup batter over bottom element of waffle iron. Close iron; cook waffle about 3 minutes, or until browned on both sides and crisp. Transfer waffle to plate; cover to keep warm. Repeat with cooking oil spray and remaining batter.
5 Serve waffles dusted with sifted confectioner's sugar and drizzled with maple syrup.

prep + cook time 45 minutes **makes** 12
nutritional count per waffle 15.8 g total fat (2.9 g saturated fat); 388 cal; 58.1 g carbohydrate; 3 g protein; 0.8 g fiber
storage Waffles can be frozen in an airtight container for up to 3 months. Reheat waffles in the oven.

7 ozs dairy-free spread
¾ cup superfine sugar
1 teaspoon vanilla extract
3 large eggs, separated
1¼ cups potato flour
1 cup brown rice flour
1 teaspoon gluten-free
   baking powder
1 cup water
cooking-oil spray
2 teaspoons confectioner's
   sugar
1 cup pure maple syrup

toasted granola

This recipe is gluten-free, wheat-free, yeast-free, and egg-free.

. . . .

2 tablespoons golden syrup

2 tablespoons macadamia oil

1 cup gluten-free cornflakes

1 cup rolled rice

1 cup puffed rice

1 cup coarsely
  chopped macadamias

1 cup coarsely
  chopped pistachios

1 cup coarsely
  chopped almond kernels

½ cup flaked coconut

½ cup finely chopped dried figs

½ cup dried cranberries

1 Preheat oven to 350°F/325°F convection.

2 Combine syrup and oil in small bowl.

3 Combine cornflakes, rolled rice, puffed rice, nuts, and coconut in shallow baking dish; drizzle with syrup mixture. Roast, uncovered, about 15 minutes, or until browned lightly, stirring halfway through roasting time. Cool 10 minutes.

4 Stir fruit into granola mixture; cool.

prep + cook time 25 minutes (+ cooling)

makes 8 cups or **serves** 24 (⅓ cup per serving)

nutritional count per serving 2.7 g total fat (2.1 g saturated fat); 194 cal; 13.5 g carbohydrate; 3.7 g protein; 2.7 g fiber

storage Store granola in an airtight container in the refrigerator for up to one month.

apple & ricotta fritters

This recipe is gluten-free, wheat-free, and yeast-free.

- -

1 Combine ricotta, sifted flour, sugar, nutmeg, egg, and apple in medium bowl.

2 Heat 2 inches of oil in large saucepan; deep-fry rounded tablespoons of ricotta mixture, in batches, until browned lightly. Drain on paper towels. Toss fritters in combined extra sugar and cinnamon.

3 Serve fritters with maple syrup drizzled over them.

prep + cook time 25 minutes **makes** 24

nutritional count per fritter 3.8 g total fat (1.5 g saturated fat); 85 cal; 10.3 g carbohydrate; 2.2 g protein; 0.2 g fiber

1¾ cups ricotta cheese

⅔ cup gluten-free
self-rising flour

2 tablespoons superfine sugar

½ teaspoon ground nutmeg

1 egg

1 large apple, peeled, finely
chopped

vegetable oil, for deep-frying

⅓ cup superfine sugar, extra

1 teaspoon ground cinnamon

2 tablespoons pure maple
syrup

rolled rice porridge

This recipe is gluten-free, wheat-free, yeast-free, dairy-free, egg-free, and nut-free.

• •

1½ cups rolled rice

4½ cups water

⅓ cup rice milk

⅓ cup coarsely chopped dried apricots

¼ cup flaked coconut, toasted

2 tablespoons honey

1 Combine rolled rice and 3 cups of the water in medium bowl. Cover; let stand at room temperature overnight.

2 Place undrained rolled rice in medium saucepan; cook, stirring, until mixture comes to the boil. Add the remaining water; bring to the boil. Reduce heat; simmer, uncovered, for about 5 minutes, or until thickened.

3 Divide porridge and milk among serving bowls. Garnish with apricots and coconut; drizzle the honey over the top.

prep + cook time 20 minutes (+ standing) **serves** 4

nutritional count per serving 2.8 g total fat (1.7 g saturated fat); 252 cal; 50.7 g carbohydrate; 3.9 g protein; 2.7 g fiber

tip You can substitute soy, whole, or skim milk for the rice milk.

banana hotcakes

This recipe is gluten-free, wheat-free, yeast-free, and nut-free.

1 Sift flours and sugar into medium bowl. Whisk milk, eggs, and half the butter in medium bowl. Gradually whisk milk mixture into flour mixture until smooth.

2 Heat large heavy frying pan over medium heat; brush with a little of the remaining butter. Pour 2 tablespoons batter for each pancake into heated pan (you can cook three at a time). Cook pancakes until bubbles appear on the surface; top pancakes with banana, sprinkle each pancake with a rounded teaspoon of brown sugar. Turn pancakes, cook until sugar has caramelized and banana is browned lightly. Cover to keep warm.

3 Repeat process using remaining melted butter, batter, banana, and brown sugar, wiping out pan between batches.

prep + cook time 25 minutes **makes** 12

nutritional count per hotcake 5.1 g total fat (2.8 g saturated fat); 179 cal; 29.3 g carbohydrate; 3.3 g protein; 0.9 g fiber

goes well with extra fresh sliced banana and maple syrup.

1¼ cups gluten-free
   self-rising flour
¼ cup brown rice flour
2 tablespoons superfine sugar
1 cup milk
3 large eggs
3 tablespoons butter, melted
2 large bananas, thickly sliced
¼ cup light brown sugar

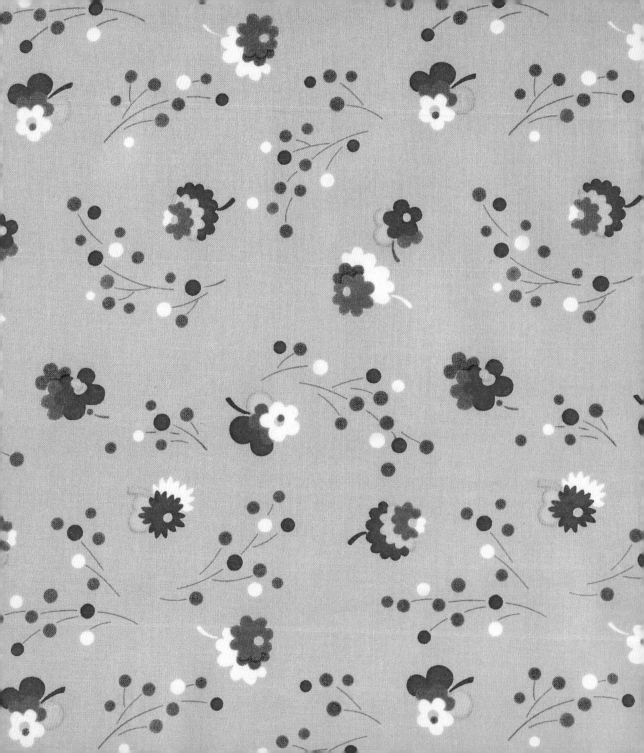

the lunchbox

Lunch, particularly when you're at work or school, presents the biggest problems when you're gluten-intolerant – no sandwiches. These delicious lunchbox solutions will make you the envy of your friends.

rice noodle cakes

This recipe is gluten-free, wheat-free, yeast-free, dairy-free, and nut-free.

1 Place noodles in large heatproof bowl; cover with boiling water. Let stand 5 minutes, or until tender; drain. Cut noodles coarsely with scissors.

2 Combine noodles, egg, carrot, zucchini, coriander, and chili sauce in large bowl.

3 Heat a little of the oil in large frying pan; cook ¼-cup noodle mixture, flattening slightly with spatula, until browned on both sides. Repeat with remaining oil and noodle mixture, cooking three or four cakes at a time.

4 Serve noodle cakes with extra sweet chili sauce.

prep + cook time 35 minutes **makes** 20

nutritional count per cake 2.8 g total fat (0.5 g saturated fat); 63 cal; 7.2 g carbohydrate; 1.8 g protein; 0.5 g fiber

storage Store cooked rice noodle cakes in an airtight container in the refrigerator for up to 3 days or freeze for up to 3 months. Rice noodle cakes can be eaten cold or reheated in the microwave on high (100%) for about 30 seconds.

7 ozs rice vermicelli noodles
3 large eggs, beaten lightly
1 medium carrot, coarsely grated
1 medium zucchini, coarsely grated
½ cup coarsely chopped fresh coriander (cilantro)
2 tablespoons gluten-free sweet chili sauce
2 tablespoons vegetable oil

zucchini, olive & tomato polenta fingers

This recipe is gluten-free, wheat-free, yeast-free, egg-free, and nut-free.

2 cups water
2 cups gluten-free chicken
  stock
1 cup polenta (cornmeal)
1 large zucchini,
  coarsely grated
½ cup coarsely chopped pitted
  black olives
⅓ cup finely grated
  parmesan cheese
¼ cup sun-dried tomatoes in
  oil, drained, finely chopped
2 tablespoons olive oil

1 Oil a deep 7-in-square cake pan; line base and sides with parchment paper.

2 Bring the water and stock to a boil in large saucepan; gradually stir in polenta. Reduce heat; simmer, stirring, about 10 minutes, or until polenta thickens. Stir in zucchini, olives, cheese, and tomato. Spread polenta mixture into pan; cover, refrigerate about 1 hour, or until polenta is firm.

3 Invert polenta onto board; cut in half. Cut each half into six slices.

4 Heat oil in large frying pan; cook polenta, until browned on both sides.

prep + cook time 25 minutes (+ refrigeration) **makes** 12
nutritional count per finger 4.5 g total fat (1 g saturated fat); 105 cal; 12.7 g carbohydrate; 2.9 g protein; 1.1 g fiber
storage Cooked polenta fingers can be stored in an airtight container in the refrigerator for up to 3 days. Polenta fingers can be eaten cold or reheated in the microwave on high (100%) for 30 seconds.

omelette wrap

This recipe is gluten-free, wheat-free, yeast-free, and nut-free.

1 Spray medium frying pan with cooking oil; cook half the eggs over medium heat, swirling pan to make a thin omelette. Remove from pan; cool on a parchment-paper-covered wire rack. Repeat with remaining half of eggs.
2 Combine mayonnaise, dill, and lemon juice in small bowl.
3 Spread each omelette with half of the mayonnaise mixture; top with watercress, salmon, and cucumber. Roll omelette to enclose filling.
prep + cook time 15 minutes (+ cooling) **makes** 2
nutritional count per wrap 20.8 total fat (4.5 g saturated fat); 313 cal; 5.2 g carbohydrate; 25.9 g protein; 1.4 g fiber
tip The omelette and mayonnaise mixture can be made the night before and stored, covered, in the refrigerator until ready to assemble the next day.

cooking-oil spray
4 large eggs, beaten lightly
2 tablespoons gluten-free mayonnaise
2 teaspoons finely chopped fresh dill
1 teaspoon lemon juice
3 ozs watercress, trimmed
3 ozs smoked salmon
½ lebanese cucumber, seeded, cut into matchsticks

pizza pinwheels

This recipe is gluten-free, wheat-free, yeast-free, and nut-free.

1 stick butter, softened

1 tablespoon confectioner's
sugar

2 large egg yolks

1 cup cooked mashed potato,
sieved

1 cup potato flour

½ cup brown rice flour

1 tablespoon gluten-free
baking powder

⅓ cup tomato paste

4 ozs gluten-free shaved ham,
chopped finely

1 oz baby spinach leaves

1½ cups grated pizza cheese

1 Preheat oven to 425°F/400°F convection. Oil a 7 x 11-in cookie sheet.
2 Beat butter, sifted sugar, and yolks in small bowl with electric mixer until light and fluffy. Transfer mixture to large bowl; stir in potato.
3 Stir in sifted dry ingredients to make a soft dough. Knead dough lightly on floured surface until smooth. Roll dough between sheets of parchment paper to an 8 x 12-in rectangle.
4 Spread tomato paste over dough; sprinkle the ham, spinach, and 1 cup of the cheese evenly over the dough.
5 Starting from long side, roll dough tightly, using paper as a guide; trim ends. Cut roll into 12 slices; place pinwheels, cut-side up, in single layer, on baking sheet. Bake 20 minutes. Remove pinwheels from oven, top with remaining cheese; bake further 10 minutes.
6 Serve pinwheels warm or cold.

prep + cook time 50 minutes **makes** 12
nutritional count per pinwheel 13.4 g total fat (8 g saturated fat); 230 cal; 19.7 g carbohydrate; 7.4 g protein; 1.1 g fiber
storage Pinwheels can be stored in an airtight container in the refrigerator overnight or freezer for up to 3 months.

indian vegetable fritters

This recipe is gluten-free, wheat-free, yeast-free, egg-free, and dairy-free (unless served with yogurt).

1 Using your hands, combine flour, carrot, onion, peas, garlic, spices, baking powder, coriander, and the water in medium bowl.
2 Heat 2 inches of oil in wok; deep-fry level tablespoons of vegetable mixture, in batches, until browned lightly and cooked through. Remove with a slotted spoon; drain on paper towels.
3 Fritters can be served with natural yogurt.

prep + cook time 45 minutes **makes** 36

nutritional count per fritter 2 g total fat (0.3 g saturated fat); 51 cal; 5.8 g carbohydrate; 2.2 g protein; 1.6 g fiber

storage Fritters can be stored in an airtight container in the refrigerator for up to 3 days. Eat cold or reheat fritters in the microwave on high (100%) for about 20 seconds.

2 cups chickpea flour
2 large carrots,
   coarsely grated
1 large yellow onion,
   thinly sliced
1 cup frozen peas
2 cloves garlic, crushed
1 teaspoon ground cumin
1 teaspoon garam masala
¼ teaspoon ground turmeric
½ teaspoon gluten-free
   baking powder
⅓ cup coarsely chopped
   fresh coriander (cilantro)
¼ cup water
vegetable oil, for deep-frying
natural yogurt, if desired

potato & oregano pizza

This recipe is gluten-free, wheat-free, yeast-free, dairy-free, and nut-free.

. . . .

1 (13-oz) packet gluten-free
   bread mix
11 ozs baby new potatoes,
   thinly sliced
2 teaspoons finely chopped
   fresh oregano
2 teaspoons olive oil
1 clove garlic, crushed

1 Preheat oven to 425°F/400°F convection. Oil two 10 x 14-in jelly roll pans; line bases with parchment paper, extending paper 2 inches over long sides.

2 Make bread mix according to packet directions; spread mixture into pans.

3 Combine remaining ingredients in medium bowl; spread potato mixture over bread mix.

4 Bake pizzas about 20 minutes, or until potato is tender and crusts are crisp.

prep + cook time 45 minutes **serves** 6

nutritional count per serving 2.3 g total fat (0.4 g saturated fat); 267 cal; 40.9 g carbohydrate; 8.1 g protein; 2.8 g fiber

storage Pizza slices can be stored in an airtight container in the refrigerator for up to 2 days. Pizza slices can be eaten cold or reheated in the microwave on high (100%) for about 30 seconds.

beef lasagna

This recipe is gluten-free, wheat-free, yeast-free, dairy-free, egg-free and nut-free.

1 Heat oil in large frying pan; cook onion, celery, zucchini, carrot, and garlic, stirring, until onion is soft. Add beef; cook, stirring, until browned. Add undrained tomatoes and paste; cook, stirring, about 10 minutes, or until sauce thickens slightly.

2 Meanwhile, make **white sauce**. Combine the water, milk, cloves, and bay leaf in medium saucepan; bring to the boil. Strain milk mixture into large heatproof bowl; discard solids. Melt spread in same saucepan; add cornstarch, cook, stirring 1 minute. Gradually add hot milk mixture, stirring constantly, until mixture boils and thickens. Stir in cheese.

3 Preheat oven to 350°F/325°F convection. Oil deep 10-cup capacity rectangular ovenproof dish.

4 Dip eight rice paper squares, one at a time, into bowl of warm water until soft; place on board covered with tea towel. Spread 1½ cups beef mixture over base of dish; top with softened rice paper sheets. Top with half of the remaining beef mixture and half of the white sauce.

5 Soften the remaining rice paper, place on top of beef mixture; top with remaining beef mixture and white sauce.

6 Bake lasagna, uncovered, about 50 minutes, or until browned lightly. Let stand 10 minutes, garnish with chives before serving.

prep + cook time 1 hour 30 minutes **serves** 6
nutritional count per serving 15.2 g total fat (4.2 g saturated fat); 355 cal; 26.9 g carbohydrate; 25.3 g protein; 4.5 g fiber
tip If you do not have an intolerance to milk products you can substitute the soy milk and water in the white sauce recipe with 2½ cups whole cows' milk.

storage Lasagna can be stored in the refrigerator overnight or freezer for up to 3 months.

2 teaspoons olive oil
1 medium yellow onion,
   finely chopped
1 trimmed celery stalk,
   finely chopped
1 small zucchini,
   finely chopped
1 small carrot,
   finely chopped
2 cloves garlic, crushed
21 ozs ground beef
1 (28-oz) can crushed tomatoes
½ cup tomato paste

white sauce

1½ cups water
1 cup gluten-free
   soy milk
2 cloves
1 bay leaf
2 tablespoons dairy-free
   spread
2 tablespoons cornstarch
3 ozs chive-flavored soy
   cheese, chopped coarsely

16 x 7-in rice paper squares
1 tablespoon finely chopped
   fresh chives

pancetta & cheese muffins

This recipe is gluten-free, wheat-free, yeast-free, and nut-free.

1 teaspoon olive oil

7 ozs gluten-free pancetta,
  finely chopped

4 green onions, thinly sliced

1¼ cups gluten-free
  self-rising flour

⅓ cup polenta (cornmeal)

¾ cup grated pizza cheese

⅔ cup milk

2 large eggs

4 tablespoons butter, melted

1 Preheat oven to 400°F/375°F convection. Line a 12-hole (⅓-cup) muffin pan with paper liners.

2 Heat oil in medium frying pan; cook pancetta, stirring, about 3 minutes, or until browned lightly. Add onion; cook, stirring, until soft. Cool.

3 Combine flour, polenta, and ½ cup of the cheese in medium bowl; stir in combined milk and eggs, melted butter, and pancetta mixture.

4 Divide mixture among paper liners; garnish with remaining cheese. Bake about 20 minutes. Let muffins stand in pan 5 minutes; turn, top-side up, onto wire rack to cool.

prep + cook time 35 minutes **makes** 12
nutritional count per muffin 9.7 g total fat (5.1 g saturated fat); 143 cal; 16.7 g carbohydrate; 7.2 g protein; 0.4 g fiber
storage Muffins can be stored in the refrigerator in an airtight container for up to 2 days or freezer for up to 3 months.

egg, bacon & parmesan pies

This recipe is gluten-free, wheat-free, and yeast-free.

- -

1 Make **pastry**. Process flours, cheese, and butter until fine. Add enough of the water to make ingredients come together. Cover; refrigerate 30 minutes.

2 Preheat oven to 425°F/400°F convection. Oil a 6-hole (¾-cup) jumbo muffin pan.

3 Roll pastry between sheets of parchment paper until ⅛-in thick; cut six 4-in rounds from pastry. Ease pastry rounds into pan holes, press into base and sides; prick bases with fork.

4 Bake pastry shells about 10 minutes, or until browned lightly. Cool pastry in pan. Reduce oven temperature to 400°F/375°F convection.

5 Meanwhile, heat oil in small frying pan; cook bacon, onion, and garlic, stirring, until bacon is soft. Divide bacon mixture among pastry shells.

6 Whisk eggs and cream in medium bowl; stir in cheese and chives. Fill pastry shells with egg mixture. Bake about 25 minutes, or until set.

prep + cook time 50 minutes (+ refrigeration and cooling) **makes** 6
nutritional count per pie 37.9 g total fat (20.8 g saturated fat); 548 cal; 54 g carbohydrate; 17.6 g protein; 1.5 g fiber
storage Pies can be stored in an airtight container in the refrigerator for up to 3 days or freezer for up to 1 month.

pastry

1 cup rice flour
¼ cup cornstarch
¼ cup soy flour
¼ cup finely grated parmesan cheese
10 tablespoons cold butter, diced
2 tablespoons cold water, approximately

2 teaspoons vegetable oil
3 strips bacon, finely chopped
1 small yellow onion, finely chopped
1 clove garlic, crushed
4 large eggs
¼ cup cream
¼ cup finely grated parmesan cheese
1 tablespoon finely chopped fresh chives

kids' parties

An allergic child can feel seriously left out at parties. These recipes for good-looking and good-tasting party food don't appear to be in the least like 'special' food. All the party guests will be coming back for more.

mini meat pies

This recipe is gluten-free, wheat-free, yeast-free, and nut-free.

. . . .

2 teaspoons vegetable oil

1 medium yellow onion,
   finely chopped

2 strips bacon, finely chopped

12 ozs ground beef

2 tablespoons tomato paste

¼ cup arrowroot

2 cups gluten-free
   beef stock

pastry

1¾ cups rice flour

⅓ cup cornstarch

⅓ cup soy flour

14 tablespoons cold butter,
   diced

¼ cup cold water,
   approximately

1 large egg, beaten lightly

gluten-free tomato sauce

1 Heat oil in medium saucepan; cook onion and bacon, stirring, until onion softens and bacon is browned. Add beef; cook, stirring, until browned. Add paste and blended arrowroot and stock; bring to the boil, stirring. Reduce heat; simmer, uncovered, until thickened. Cool.

2 Meanwhile, make **pastry**. Process flours and butter until mixture is fine. Add enough of the water to make ingredients come together. Cover; refrigerate 30 minutes.

3 Preheat oven to 425°F/400°F convection. Oil a 12 x ¼-cup mini foil pie tins (3-in-diameter top, 2-in-diameter base); place on baking sheet.

4 Roll pastry between sheets of parchment paper until ⅛-in thick; cut 12 x 3½-in rounds from pastry. Ease pastry rounds into tins; press into base and sides. Spoon beef mixture into pastry shells; brush edges with egg. Cut 12 x 3-in rounds from remaining pastry; place rounds on pies, press to seal edges. Brush pies with egg; cut two small slits in top of each pie.

5 Bake pies about 25 minutes. Serve with gluten-free tomato sauce.

prep + cook time 1 hour (+ refrigeration and standing) **makes** 12
nutritional count per pie 19.3 g total fat (11 g saturated fat);
247 cal; 7.8 g carbohydrate; 10.7 g protein; 0.7 g fiber
storage Pies can be frozen for up to 1 month.

mini pizza squares

This recipe is gluten-free, wheat-free, yeast-free, and nut-free.

1 Preheat oven to 425°F/400°F convection. Oil two 10 x 14-in jelly-roll pans; line bases with parchment paper, extending paper 2 inches over long sides.

2 Make bread mix according to packet directions; spread mixture into pans. Bake about 12 minutes, or until browned lightly. Remove from oven.

3 Spread paste over crusts. Sprinkle sliced tomato, peppers, onion, and feta over one pizza crust; sprinkle pineapple, ham, and pizza cheese over remaining pizza crust.

4 Bake pizzas, about 15 minutes, or until cheese melts and crusts are crisp. Cut each pizza into 20 squares. Top each peppers and feta pizza square with olives and basil leaves. Top each ham and pineapple pizza square with a cherry tomato quarter and an oregano leaf.

prep + cook time 50 minutes **makes** 40 squares (20 of each pizza)

nutritional count per capsicum and feta pizza square
2.5 g total fat (1.2 g saturated fat); 68 cal; 8.3 g carbohydrate; 2.8 g protein; 0.7 g fiber

nutritional count per ham and pineapple pizza square
1.4 g total fat (0.8 g saturated fat); 65 cal; 9.1 g carbohydrate; 3.6 g protein; 0.8 g fiber

13-oz packet gluten-free bread mix

⅓ cup tomato paste

2 medium tomatoes, thinly sliced

10-oz jar roasted peppers in oil, drained, coarsely chopped

½ small red onion, thinly sliced

5 ozs soft feta cheese, crumbled

1 (15-oz) can pineapple pieces, drained

3 ozs shaved gluten-free ham, coarsely chopped

1 cup pizza cheese

½ cup pitted green olives, halved

20 small fresh basil leaves

5 cherry tomatoes, quartered

20 fresh oregano leaves

crunchy chicken fingers

This recipe is gluten-free, wheat-free, yeast-free, dairy-free, and nut-free.

8 chicken tenderloins (21 ozs)
1 (3-oz) packet gluten-free
   plain potato chips
1 large egg white
⅓ cup gluten-free
   sweet chili sauce

1 Preheat oven to 400°F/375°F convection.

2 Cut tenderloins in half, diagonally.

3 Coarsely crush chips while still in the bag, place in medium shallow bowl. Whisk egg white lightly in small shallow bowl.

4 Dip chicken pieces in egg white then in chips to coat; place in single layer, on oiled wire rack over baking sheet.

5 Bake chicken fingers about 15 minutes, or until chicken is cooked through. Serve fingers with chili sauce.

prep + cook time 30 minutes **makes** 16

nutritional count per finger 4.2 g total fat (1.5 g saturated fat); 90 cal; 4 g carbohydrate; 8.7 g protein; 1 g fiber

tip Tomato sauce can be substituted for sweet chili sauce.

storage Leftover chicken fingers can be kept in the refrigerator for 1 day, and reheated in the oven.

mini corn & chive muffins

This recipe is gluten-free, wheat-free, yeast-free, and nut-free.

. . . .

1 Preheat oven to 400°F/375°F convection. Butter two 12-hole (1-tablespoon) mini muffin pans.

2 Sift flour into medium bowl; stir in butter, eggs, corn, cheese, and chives. Divide mixture among pans.

3 Bake muffins about 15 minutes. Let muffins stand in pan 5 minutes; turn out onto wire rack to cool.

prep + cook time 30 minutes **makes** 24

nutritional count per muffin 4.1 g total fat (2.5 g saturated fat); 56 cal; 8.1 g carbohydrate; 1.5 g protein; 0.5 g fiber

storage Muffins can be stored in airtight container in refrigerator for up to 2 days or freezer for up to 1 month.

1¼ cups gluten-free
  self-rising flour
6 tablespoons butter, melted,
  plus more for pan
2 large eggs, beaten lightly
2 (4-oz) cans gluten-free
  creamed corn
½ cup grated pizza cheese
2 tablespoons finely chopped
  fresh chives

blueberry bubble bark

This recipe is gluten-free, wheat-free, yeast-free, and egg-free.

. . . .

6 ozs white chocolate, melted
¾ cup puffed rice
½ cup shredded coconut
½ cup dried blueberries
¼ cup unsalted pistachios,
    coarsely chopped

1 Grease a 4 x 13-in rectangular tart pan; line base and two long sides with parchment paper, extending paper 2 inches above sides.
2 Combine all ingredients in medium bowl.
3 Spoon mixture evenly into pan; refrigerate until set. Remove bark from pan; cut into slices or break into chunks.
prep + cook time 15 minutes (+ refrigeration) **makes** 16
nutritional count per slice 6.5 g total fat (3.9 g saturated fat); 97 cal; 7.9 g carbohydrate; 1.5 g protein; 0.7 g fiber
tips You can substitute dried cranberries for the dried blueberries. Use a serrated knife for cutting the bark.
storage Bark can be stored in an airtight container in the refrigerator for up to 1 week.

chocolate & fruit crackles

This recipe is gluten-free, wheat-free, yeast-free, and egg-free.

. . . .

1 Line two 12-hole muffin tins with paper liners.
2 Combine cornflakes, rice, raisins, flour, and seeds in large bowl; stir in chocolate.
3 Divide mixture among paper liners; press down gently, sprinkle nonpareils over each. Refrigerate 1 hour, or until set.

prep + cook time 20 minutes (+ refrigeration) **makes** 24
nutritional count per crackle 4.4 g total fat (1.9 g saturated fat); 99 cal; 12.6 g carbohydrate; 1.7 g protein; 0.8 g fiber
storage Crackles can be stored in an airtight container in the refrigerator for up to 1 week.

2 cups gluten-free cornflakes
1 cup puffed rice
½ cup golden raisins
⅓ cup hazelnut flour
2 tablespoons sunflower seeds
8 ozs milk chocolate, melted
2 teaspoons gluten-free
   nonpareils

moist flourless chocolate nut cake

This recipe is gluten-free, wheat-free, and yeast-free.

½ cup cocoa powder

½ cup hot water

1½ cups firmly packed
light brown sugar

2 sticks unsalted butter,
coarsely chopped

7 ozs bittersweet chocolate,
coarsely chopped

1½ cups hazelnut flour

6 large eggs, beaten lightly

chocolate ganache

¾ cup cream

10 ozs bittersweet chocolate,
coarsely chopped

8 ozs strawberries, thinly sliced

1 Preheat oven to 350°F/325°F convection. Grease a 10-in round springform pan; line base and side with parchment paper.

2 Blend cocoa with the water in medium saucepan until smooth. Add sugar, butter, and chocolate; stir over low heat until smooth. Remove from heat.

3 Let chocolate mixture stand about 15 minutes, or until barely warm. Stir in flour and egg. Pour mixture into pan.

4 Bake cake about 1 hour 40 minutes. Cool cake in pan. Refrigerate, covered, 3 hours or overnight.

5 Meanwhile, make **chocolate ganache**. Bring cream to the boil in small saucepan. Remove from heat, add chocolate; stir until smooth. Let stand 20 minutes before using.

6 Place cake onto serving plate. Cover with ganache, decorate with strawberries.

prep + cook time 2 hours (+ cooling and refrigeration) **serves** 16
nutritional count per serving 33.2 g total fat (17.1 g saturated fat); 493 cal; 41.6 g carbohydrate; 6.7 g protein; 1.8 g fiber
tip This cake is a moist, dense, rich cake. Serve cut into slim wedges.
storage Undecorated cake can be stored in an airtight container in the refrigerator for up to 1 week, or freezer for up to 2 months.

carrot cupcakes

This recipe is gluten-free, wheat-free, yeast-free, and nut-free.

. . . .

1 Preheat oven to 350°F/325°F convection. Line a 12-hole (⅓-cup) muffin tin with paper liners.

2 Beat sugar, oil, and eggs in small bowl with electric mixer until thick and creamy. Transfer mixture to large bowl; stir in carrot, then sifted dry ingredients. Divide mixture among paper liners.

3 Bake cupcakes about 20 minutes. Let cupcakes stand in pan 5 minutes; turn, top-side up, onto wire rack to cool.

4 Increase oven temperature to 400°F/375°F convection. Grease baking sheets; line with parchment paper. Place candies on sheets, in batches of six to eight, about 2 ins apart; bake 4 minutes. Let stand on trays 2 to 3 minutes. When cool enough to handle, carefully lift shapes from trays and mold into petal shapes.

5 Make **cream cheese frosting**. Beat cream cheese and butter in small bowl with electric mixer until light and fluffy; gradually beat in sifted sugar.

6 Spread cool cakes with three-quarters of the frosting. Position petals on cakes to make flowers. Transfer remaining frosting into piping bag fitted with a star tip, pipe frosting into center of each flower; sprinkle sugar crystals over the centers.

prep + cook time 1 hour (+ cooling) **makes** 12

nutritional count per cupcake 17.5 g total fat (6 g saturated fat); 348 cal; 44.9 g carbohydrate; 2.5 g protein; 0.8 g fiber

tip You will need about 3 medium carrots for this recipe.

storage Unfrosted cupcakes can be stored in an airtight container for up to 3 days, or freezer for up to 2 months.

⅔ cup firmly packed light brown sugar
½ cup vegetable oil
2 large eggs
1½ cups firmly packed coarsely grated carrot
½ cup potato flour
¼ cup cornstarch
¼ cup rice flour
1 teaspoon gluten-free baking powder
¼ teaspoon baking soda
1 teaspoon pie spice
2 (3-oz) packets colored gluten-free sugar-free hard candies
yellow, pink, and orange sugar crystals

cream cheese frosting
8 ozs cream cheese, softened
4 tablespoons butter, softened
½ cup confectioner's sugar

passionfruit & white chocolate gelatin cake

This recipe is gluten-free, wheat-free, and yeast-free. You can use any flavored gelatin you like.

1 Oil a deep 7-in-square cake pan with hazelnut oil. Make gelatin according to packet directions; pour into pan. Refrigerate 3 hours or until set.

2 Make white chocolate ganache. Stir chocolate and cream in medium heatproof bowl over medium saucepan of simmering water until smooth. Cool.

3 Pour three-quarters of ganache over the gelatin; refrigerate 1 hour.

4 Meanwhile, preheat oven to 350°F/325°F convection. Grease a 9-in-square cake pan; line base with parchment paper.

5 Beat eggs in small bowl with electric mixer until thick and creamy. Gradually beat in sugar, beating until sugar dissolves. Fold in triple-sifted cornstarch. Spread mixture into pan.

6 Bake cake about 20 minutes. Turn cake onto parchment-paper-covered wire rack to cool.

7 Trim cake to 7-ins square; place in pan on top of ganache and jelly. Refrigerate 30 minutes.

8 Meanwhile, spread chocolate onto baking-paper-lined tray until ⅛-in thick; refrigerate about 10 minutes, or until set. Break into small pieces.

9 Place base of pan in sink of hot water for a few seconds to loosen gelatin; quickly invert cake onto serving plate. Secure chocolate pieces around edges of cake with remaining ganache; secure ribbon.

prep + cook time 40 minutes (+ refrigeration) **serves** 16
nutritional count per serving 20 g total fat (12.4 g saturated fat); 338 cal; 35.4 g carbohydrate; 4.3 g protein; 0 g fiber
storage Cake can be stored, covered, in the refrigerator for up to 2 days.

1 teaspoon hazelnut oil
1 (85-g) packet passionfruit gelatin
white chocolate ganache
12 ozs white chocolate, coarsely chopped
1¼ cups cream

3 large eggs
½ cup superfine sugar
¾ cup cornstarch
150 gs white chocolate candy melts, melted
3 feet of decorative ribbon

buttercake

This recipe is gluten-free, wheat-free, and yeast-free.

1 Preheat oven to 350°F/325°F convection. Grease and line a deep 10-in heart-shaped cake pan.

2 Beat butter in medium bowl with electric mixer until light and fluffy. Sift flour and ¼ cup of the sugar together. Beat flour mixture and milk into the butter, in two batches, only until combined.

3 Beat eggs and egg whites in small bowl with electric mixer until thick and creamy. Gradually add remaining sugar, one tablespoon at a time, beating until sugar dissolves between additions. Gradually pour egg mixture into flour mixture with motor operating on a low speed, mix only until combined.

4 Spread mixture into pan; bake about 50 minutes. Let cake stand 10 minutes; turn, top-side up, onto wire rack to cool.

5 Make **fluffy frosting**. Stir sugar and the water in small saucepan over heat, without boiling, until sugar is dissolved. Boil, uncovered, without stirring about 5 minutes, or until syrup reaches 240°F on a candy thermometer. Syrup should be thick but not colored. Remove from heat; allow bubbles to subside. Beat egg whites in small bowl with electric mixer until soft peaks form. While mixer is operating, add hot syrup in thin stream; beat on high speed about 10 minutes, or until mixture is thick and cool. Reserve 2 tablespoons of the frosting in small bowl; tint frosting green. Tint remaining frosting pink.

6 Spread top and sides of cake with pink fluffy frosting; decorate cake with roses. Spoon green fluffy frosting into small piping bag; pipe leaves onto cake.

prep + cook time 1 hour 15 minutes **serves** 12

nutritional count per serving 15.1 g total fat (9.5 g saturated fat); 325 cal; 61.4 g carbohydrate; 3.1 g protein; 0.4 g fiber

tip For a dairy-free version of this cake, substitute dairy-free spread for the butter and soy milk for the milk.

storage Cake can be stored in an airtight container for up to 2 days. Undecorated cake can be frozen for up to 3 months.

14 tablespoons butter, softened
2¼ cups gluten-free self-rising flour
1 cup superfine sugar
½ cup milk
2 large eggs
2 large egg whites
fluffy frosting
1 cup superfine sugar
½ cup water
2 large egg whites
green and pink food coloring

3 (⅓-oz) packets gluten-free edible sugar roses

baking

Cakes, cookies, and pastries all seem to be out of reach if you're gluten-intolerant. The 28 sensational recipes in this chapter will delightfully prove how mistaken you are.

mandarin, macadamia & polenta cakes

This recipe is gluten-free, wheat-free, and yeast-free.

1 Place whole mandarins in medium saucepan, cover with cold water; bring to the boil. Drain then repeat process twice. Cool mandarins to room temperature.

2 Preheat oven to 350°F/325°F convection. Line three 6-hole (⅓-cup) muffin tins with paper liners.

3 Blend or process nuts until finely chopped; place in small bowl. Halve mandarins; discard seeds. Blend or process mandarins until pulpy.

4 Beat butter and sugar in small bowl with electric mixer until light and fluffy. Beat in eggs, one at a time. Transfer mixture to large bowl; stir in polenta, baking powder, nuts, and mandarin pulp. Divide mixture among paper liners.

5 Bake cakes about 35 minutes. Let stand 5 minutes before turning, top-side up, onto wire rack to cool.

6 Meanwhile, make **mandarin icing**. Sift confectioner's sugar into small bowl, stir in juice and butter.

7 Spread cool cakes with mandarin icing. Decorate with flowers.

prep + cook time 1 hour 15 minutes (+ cooling) **makes** 18
nutritional count per cake 25.3 g total fat (10 g saturated fat); 379 cal; 34.4 g carbohydrate; 3.3 g protein; 1.5 g fiber
storage Cakes can be stored in an airtight container for up to 3 days.

4 small whole mandarin oranges
2 cups untoasted unsalted macadamias
2 sticks butter, softened
1 cup superfine sugar
3 large eggs
1 cup polenta (corn meal)
1 teaspoon gluten-free baking powder

mandarin icing
1½ cups confectioner's sugar
2 tablespoons mandarin juice
1½ tablespoons softened butter

gluten-free edible sugar flowers

orange & ginger florentines

This recipe is gluten-free, wheat-free, yeast-free, and egg-free.

2 medium oranges

½ cup superfine sugar

½ cup water

2 tablespoons finely chopped
  candied ginger

2 cups gluten-free
  rice flakes

¾ cup sliced almonds

⅔ cup sweetened condensed
  milk

4 ozs bittersweet chocolate
  (70% cocoa solids), melted

1 Using vegetable peeler, peel orange rind from oranges; slice rind thinly. Cook rind in small saucepan of boiling water for 2 minutes; drain.

2 Return rind to small saucepan with sugar and the ½ cup water; stir over heat until sugar dissolves. Bring to the boil. Boil, uncovered, 5 minutes; transfer rind from pan to wire rack, discard syrup.

3 Preheat oven to 400°F/375°F convection. Grease baking sheets; line with parchment paper.

4 Combine rind, ginger, rice flakes, nuts, and milk in medium bowl. Drop level tablespoons of mixture onto sheets, allowing 2 inches between each florentine.

5 Bake florentines about 6 minutes, or until browned lightly. Cool on trays.

6 Spread the bases of the florentines with chocolate; run fork through chocolate to make wave pattern. Set at room temperature.

prep + cook time 40 minutes (+ standing) **makes** 22
nutritional count per florentine 3.8 g total fat (1.5 g saturated fat); 96 cal; 13.3 g carbohydrate; 2 g protein; 0.5 g fiber
storage Florentines can be stored in an airtight container for up to 2 weeks.

apple & pear crumble

This recipe is gluten-free, wheat-free, yeast-free, and egg-free.

. . . .

1 Preheat oven to 350°F/325°F convection. Grease a deep 6-cup ovenproof dish.

2 Peel, core, and quarter apples and pears; thickly slice fruit. Combine fruit, sugar, and the water in large saucepan; cook, covered, about 10 minutes, or until fruit is just tender. Drain; discard liquid.

3 Meanwhile, make **crumble topping**. Blend or process ingredients until combined.

4 Place apple mixture in dish; sprinkle topping over the top. Bake crumble about 25 minutes.

prep + cook time 45 minutes **serves** 4

nutritional count per serving 21 g total fat (8.7 g saturated fat); 522 cal; 75.2 g carbohydrate; 4.8 g protein; 5.8 g fiber
variations

granola crumble Prepare half the amount of basic crumble mixture; stir in 1 cup toasted granola (see page 15).

coconut crumble Prepare half the amount of basic crumble mixture; stir in ½-cup shredded coconut.

3 medium apples
3 medium pears
¼ cup superfine sugar
¼ cup water
crumble topping
½ cup almond flour
⅓ cup rice flour
⅓ cup firmly packed light
  brown sugar
4 tablespoons butter, chopped
1 teaspoon ground cinnamon

chocolate pecan cookies

This recipe is gluten-free, wheat-free, and yeast-free.

1½ cups pecan pieces

1 stick butter, softened

½ cup superfine sugar

½ teaspoon vanilla extract

1 large egg

⅔ cup brown rice flour

½ cup cornstarch

5 ozs bittersweet chocolate,
  coarsely chopped

24 whole pecans

2 ozs bittersweet chocolate,
  melted

1 Preheat oven to 350°F/325°F convection. Grease baking sheets; line with parchment paper.

2 Process pecan pieces until ground finely.

3 Beat butter, sugar, vanilla, and pecan meal in small bowl with electric mixer until light and fluffy. Add egg; beat until combined. Stir in sifted flours, then chopped chocolate.

4 Roll rounded tablespoons of mixture into balls; place 3 ins apart on trays, flatten slightly. Top with whole pecans.

5 Bake cookies about 20 minutes. Cool on trays.

6 Drizzle melted chocolate over cookies.

prep + cook time 55 minutes (+ cooling) **makes** 24

nutritional count per cookie 12.8 g total fat (4.7 g saturated fat); 186 cal; 15.8 g carbohydrate; 1.8 g protein; 0.8 g fiber

storage Cookies can be stored in an airtight container for up to 1 week.

raspberry cheesecake

This recipe is gluten-free, wheat-free, and yeast-free. To ensure recipe is also nut-free, check the label on the coconut packets to ensure they do not contain traces of nuts.

1 Preheat oven to 350°F/325°F convection. Grease a deep 7-in-square cake pan; line base and sides with parchment paper, extending paper 2 inches above edges.

2 Beat egg whites lightly in medium bowl, stir in coconuts and sugar; press mixture firmly over base of pan.

3 Bake base about 15 minutes, or until browned lightly. Cool.

4 Meanwhile, sprinkle gelatin over the water in small heatproof bowl; let bowl stand in small saucepan of simmering water. Stir until gelatin dissolves. Cool 5 minutes.

5 Beat cheese and extra sugar in medium bowl with electric mixer until smooth; beat in cream and vanilla. Stir in gelatin mixture.

6 Sprinkle half the raspberries over base; pour in filling. Blend or process remaining raspberries; strain. Drizzle raspberry puree over cheesecake, pull skewer backwards and forwards several times for marbled effect. Refrigerate 3 hours or overnight.

prep + cook time 35 minutes (+ refrigeration) **serves** 12
nutritional count per serving 31.2 g total fat (21.7 g saturated fat); 384 cal; 19.4 g carbohydrate; 6 g protein; 2.8 g fiber
storage Slice can be stored, covered, in the refrigerator.

2 large egg whites
¾ cup desiccated coconut
¾ cup shredded coconut
⅓ cup superfine sugar
3 teaspoons powdered
    unflavored gelatin
¼ cup water
18 ozs cream cheese, softened
½ cup superfine sugar, extra
1¼ cups cream
1 teaspoon vanilla extract
11 ozs raspberries

berry frangipane tarts

This recipe is gluten-free, wheat-free, and yeast-free.

. . . .

5 tablespoons butter, softened
½ teaspoon vanilla extract
⅓ cup superfine sugar
1 large egg
¾ cup almond flour
1 tablespoon cornstarch
5 ozs fresh blueberries and
   raspberries
1 tablespoon confectioner's
   sugar

1 Preheat oven to 350°F/325°F convection. Grease six 2 x 4-in removable-bottom tart pans; place on baking sheet.
2 Beat butter, vanilla, and superfine sugar in small bowl with electric mixer until light and fluffy. Add egg; beat until combined. Stir in flour and cornstarch. Spoon mixture into pans; smooth surface, sprinkle berries over the top.
3 Bake tarts about 30 minutes. Let stand in pans 10 minutes; turn carefully, top-side up, onto parchment-paper-covered wire rack.
4 Serve tarts warm or cold, dusted with sifted confectioner's sugar.
prep + cook time 45 minutes **makes** 6
nutritional count per tart 19.5 g total fat (7.6 g saturated fat); 271 cal; 18.8 g carbohydrate; 4.4 g protein; 2.2 g fiber
storage Tarts can be stored in an airtight container for up to 2 days.

passionfruit kisses

This recipe is gluten-free, wheat-free, yeast-free, and dairy-free.

. . . .

1 Preheat oven to 350°F/325°F convection. Grease four 12-hole (1½-tablespoons) round-based patty pans or jumbo muffin tins.
2 Beat eggs in small bowl with electric mixer until thick and creamy. Add superfine sugar, one tablespoon at a time, beating until sugar dissolves between additions. Gently fold in triple-sifted cornstarch. Drop one level tablespoon of mixture into each pan hole.
3 Bake cakes about 10 minutes. Turn cakes immediately onto parchment-paper-covered wire rack by tapping upside-down pans firmly on the counter to release the cakes; cool.
4 Meanwhile, make **passionfruit filling**. Beat spread in small bowl with electric mixer until as white as possible; gradually beat in sifted confectioner's sugar. Stir in passionfruit.
5 Sandwich cool kisses with passionfruit filling; serve dusted with sifted confectioner's sugar.

prep + cook time 40 minutes (+ cooling) **makes** 24
nutritional count per kiss 3.7 g total fat (0.7 g saturated fat); 116 cal; 19.5 g carbohydrate; 0.9 g protein; 0.3 g fiber
storage Kisses can be stored in an airtight container for 1 day. Unfilled kisses can be frozen for up to 3 months.

3 large eggs
½ cup superfine sugar
¾ cup cornstarch
passionfruit filling

3 ozs dairy-free spread
1½ cups confectioner's sugar
2 tablespoons passionfruit pulp

2 tablespoons confectioner's
   sugar

chocolate fudge brownies

This recipe is gluten-free, wheat-free, and yeast-free.

. . . .

10 tablespoons butter, coarsely
   chopped
10½ ozs bittersweet chocolate,
   chopped coarsely
1½ cups firmly packed
   light brown sugar
3 large eggs
¾ cup hazelnut flour
½ cup buckwheat flour
½ cup sour cream
¼ cup cocoa powder

1 Preheat oven to 350°F/325°F convection. Grease a 7 x 11-in high-sided baking sheet; line base with parchment paper, extending paper 2 ins over two long sides.

2 Melt butter and chocolate in medium saucepan over low heat. Stir in sugar; cook, stirring, 2 minutes. Cool 10 minutes.

3 Stir in eggs, then flours, sour cream, and 2 tablespoons of the sifted cocoa powder. Spread mixture into pan.

4 Bake brownies about 45 minutes. Cool in pan before cutting into squares. Serve dusted with remaining sifted cocoa.

prep + cook time 1 hour 10 minutes (+ cooling) **makes** 18
nutritional count per brownie 18 g total fat (9.6 g saturated fat); 305 cal; 32 g carbohydrate; 3.6 g protein; 0.8 g fiber
storage Brownies can be stored in an airtight container in the refrigerator for up to 4 days.

chocolate apple cake

This recipe is gluten-free, wheat-free, yeast-free, and dairy-free.

. . . .

1 Preheat oven to 350°F/325°F convection. Grease a 8 x 12-in high-sided baking sheet; line base with parchment paper, extending paper 2 inches over two long sides.

2 Peel apples; coarsely grate. Chop grated apple finely.

3 Sift dry ingredients into large bowl; stir in apple, flour, eggs, oil, and vanilla. Pour mixture into pan.

4 Bake cake about 45 minutes. Turn, top-side up, onto wire rack to cool.

5 Meanwhile, make **chocolate icing**. Sift sugar and cocoa into small bowl; stir in enough juice to make a thick icing.

6 Spread chocolate icing on cool cake.

prep + cook time 1 hour 10 minutes (+ cooling) **serves** 18
nutritional count per serving 15 g total fat (2.2 g saturated fat); 285 cal; 34.7 g carbohydrate; 2.6 g protein; 1.3 g fiber
tip Use a hot dry knife to cut the cake.
storage Cake can be stored in an airtight container for up to 3 days. Un-iced cake can be frozen for up to 3 months.

4 medium apples
¾ cup potato flour
¾ cup brown rice flour
¼ cup cocoa powder
1 cup superfine sugar
1 teaspoon baking soda
¼ cup linseed flour (flax meal)
4 large eggs, beaten lightly
1 cup vegetable oil
1 teaspoon vanilla extract
chocolate icing
1 cup confectioner's sugar
1 tablespoon cocoa powder
2 tablespoons apple juice, approximately

sweet potato biscuits

This recipe is gluten-free, wheat-free, yeast-free, and egg-free.

· ·

1⅔ cups gluten-free
   self-rising flour
1 teaspoon superfine sugar
¼ teaspoon salt
1½ tablespoons butter
½ cup cold mashed sieved
   cooked sweet potato
½ cup buttermilk
2 tablespoons water,
   approximately
2 teaspoons milk,
   approximately
2 teaspoons gluten-free
   self-rising flour, extra

1 Preheat oven to 425°F/400°F convection. Oil baking sheet.
2 Sift dry ingredients into large bowl; rub in the butter. Add sweet potato, buttermilk, and enough of the water to mix to a soft, sticky dough. Knead dough lightly on floured surface until smooth.
3 Divide dough into four equal portions. Roll each portion into rounds, place on baking sheet. Cut cross through top of dough, about 2 inches deep. Brush tops with milk, then dust with extra sifted flour.
4 Bake biscuits about 35 minutes.

prep + cook time 50 minutes **makes** 4
nutritional count per biscuit 5.2 g total fat (3.2 g saturated fat); 130 cal; 56.5 g carbohydrate; 2.8 g protein; 1.5 g fiber
tip You will need to cook 8oz sweet potato for this recipe.
storage Biscuits are best made and eaten on the same day. They can be frozen for up to 3 months. Thaw in the oven, wrapped in foil.

lime curd meringue tarts

This recipe is gluten-free, wheat-free, yeast-free, and dairy-free.

· ·

1 Preheat oven to 250°F/225°F convection. Line a 6-hole (⅓-cup) muffin tin with paper liners.

2 Beat egg whites in small bowl with electric mixer until soft peaks form; gradually add sugars, one tablespoon at a time, beating until sugar dissolves between additions.

3 Spoon meringue into paper liners; using the back of a metal spoon, make a small hollow in each meringue.

4 Bake meringues about 1 hour; cool in oven with door ajar.

5 Meanwhile, make **lime curd**. Strain eggs into medium heatproof bowl, stir in sugar, spread, and juice; stir over medium saucepan of simmering water until mixture thickens and coats the back of a wooden spoon. Remove from heat. Let bowl stand in sink of cold water, stirring occasionally, about 10 minutes, or until cool. Stir in rind and tint with food coloring. Cover; refrigerate 1 hour, or until thick.

6 Serve meringues topped with curd, then mint leaves. Dust with extra sifted confectioner's sugar.

prep + cook time 1 hour 15 minutes (+ refrigeration) **makes** 6
nutritional count per meringue 13.9 g total fat (2.7 g saturated fat); 293 cal; 38.4 g carbohydrate; 3.6 g protein; 0.9 g fiber
tip You will need about 3 limes for this recipe.
storage Meringues are best made and eaten on the same day. Top meringues with curd just before serving.

2 large egg whites
½ cup superfine sugar
2 teaspoons confectioner's sugar

lime curd
2 large eggs, beaten lightly
½ cup superfine sugar
3 ozs dairy-free spread
⅓ cup lime juice
2 teaspoons finely grated lime rind
green food coloring

6 fresh mint leaves
1 teaspoon confectioner's sugar, extra

chocolate strawberry tart

This recipe is gluten-free, wheat-free, and yeast-free.

. . . .

hazelnut crust

1½ cups hazelnut flour

⅓ cup superfine sugar

¼ cup cornstarch

1 stick cold unsalted butter, chopped

1 large egg yolk

⅓ cup strawberry jam

⅔ cup cream

2 tablespoons unsalted butter

7 ozs bittersweet chocolate, finely chopped

6 strawberries, halved

1 Make **hazelnut crust**. Process flour, sugar, cornstarch, and butter until crumbly; add egg yolk, pulse until mixture comes together. Knead dough gently on floured surface until smooth. Wrap in plastic; refrigerate 1 hour.

2 Grease a 9-in-round removable-bottom tart pan. Roll hazelnut dough between sheets of parchment paper until large enough to line pan. Ease dough into pan, press into base and side; trim edge. Cover; refrigerate 30 minutes.

3 Preheat oven to 400°F/375°F convection.

4 Place pan on baking sheet. Bake hazelnut crust about 25 minutes. Spread jam over crust; return to oven 2 minutes. Cool.

5 Heat cream in medium saucepan; remove from heat, stir in butter and chocolate, then whisk until smooth. Pour chocolate mixture into crust; refrigerate 2 hours. Top tart with strawberries.

prep + cook time 50 minutes (+ refrigeration) **serves** 12
nutritional count per serving 29.1 g total fat (14 g saturated fat); 382 cal; 26.6 g carbohydrate; 3.4 g protein; 1.8 g fiber
storage Tart can be stored in an airtight container in the refrigerator, for up to 2 days.

coconut custard tarts

This recipe is gluten-free, wheat-free, and yeast-free.

1 Preheat oven to 350°F/325°F convection. Grease a 12-hole (⅓-cup) muffin tin.

2 Combine coconuts and sugar in large bowl; stir in egg whites. Press mixture over base and side of pan holes to make shells.

3 Whisk egg yolks, extra sugar, and arrowroot together in medium saucepan; gradually whisk in milk and cream to make custard.

4 Split vanilla bean in half lengthwise; scrape seeds into custard, discard pod. Add lemon rind to custard; stir over medium heat until mixture boils and thickens slightly. Remove from heat immediately; discard rind.

5 Spoon warm custard into pastry shells; bake about 15 minutes, or until set and browned lightly. Let tarts stand in pan for 10 minutes. Transfer to wire rack to cool.

6 Serve tarts dusted with sifted confectioner's sugar.

prep + cook time 45 minutes (+ standing and cooling) **makes** 12
nutritional count per tart 19.3 g total fat (15.1 g saturated fat); 295 cal; 25.4 g carbohydrate; 3.9 g protein; 2.9 g fiber
storage Tarts can be stored in an airtight container in the refrigerator for up to 2 days.

1½ cups desiccated coconut
1½ cups shredded coconut
⅔ cup superfine sugar
4 large egg whites,
    beaten lightly
3 large egg yolks
½ cup superfine sugar, extra
1 tablespoon arrowroot
¾ cup milk
½ cup cream
1 vanilla bean
1 (2-in) strip lemon rind
1 tablespoon confectioner's
    sugar

self-saucing jaffa pudding

This recipe is gluten-free, wheat-free, yeast-free, egg-free, and nut-free.

. . . .

4 tablespoons butter

½ cup milk

½ teaspoon vanilla extract

¾ cup superfine sugar

½ cup rice flour

⅓ cup soy flour

⅓ cup gluten-free
self-rising flour

1 teaspoon gluten-free
baking powder

2 tablespoons cocoa powder

2 teaspoons finely grated
orange rind

½ cup firmly packed light
brown sugar

2 cups boiling water

1 Preheat oven to 350°F/325°F convection. Grease a 6-cup ovenproof dish.

2 Melt butter with milk and vanilla in medium saucepan. Remove from heat; whisk in sugar, then sifted flours, baking powder, half the cocoa, and rind. Spread mixture into dish.

3 Sift brown sugar and the remaining cocoa over mixture; gently pour the boiling water over mixture.

4 Bake pudding about 40 minutes. Let stand 5 minutes before serving.

prep + cook time 1 hour **serves** 6

nutritional count per serving 11 g total fat (6.4 g saturated fat); 375 cal; 68.1 g carbohydrate; 4.8 g protein; 1.3 g fiber

storage Pudding can be stored in an airtight container in the refrigerator for up to 2 days.

lime & coconut cakes

This recipe is gluten-free, wheat-free, yeast-free, and nut-free.

. . . .

1 Preheat oven 400°F/375°F convection. Grease a 12-hole (½-cup) cake pan or muffin tin.

2 Whisk egg whites in large bowl with fork until combined. Add butter, flour, desiccated coconut, sifted sugar and flour, rind, and juice; stir until combined. Divide mixture among pan holes.

3 Bake cakes for 10 minutes. Remove pan from oven, sprinkle with flaked coconut; bake further 10 minutes. Let stand in pan 5 minutes; turn, top-side up, onto wire rack to cool.

prep + cook time 30 minutes (+ cooling) **makes** 12
nutritional count per cake 18.6 g total fat (11.1 g saturated fat); 280 cal; 23.6 g carbohydrate; 4.8 g protein; 3 g fiber
tip If the coconut is browning too quickly, cover the cakes loosely with foil.

storage Cakes can be stored in an airtight container for up to 3 days.

6 large egg whites
13 tablespoons butter, melted
¾ cup linseed flour (flax meal)
½ cup desiccated coconut
1½ cups confectioner's sugar
⅓ cup soy flour
2 teaspoons finely grated
  lime rind
2 tablespoons lime juice
¼ cup flaked coconut

coconut rice puddings

This recipe is gluten-free, wheat-free, yeast-free, and dairy-free.

4 large eggs

⅓ cup superfine sugar

1 teaspoon vanilla extract

1 (13½-oz) can coconut cream

1½ cups gluten-free
soy milk

1 cup cooked white
medium-grain rice

½ cup golden raisins

½ teaspoon ground cinnamon

1 Preheat oven to 350°F/325°F convection. Grease six ¾-cup ovenproof dishes.

2 Whisk eggs, sugar, and vanilla in large bowl until combined; whisk in cream and soy milk. Stir in rice and raisins. Divide mixture evenly among dishes; place dishes in large baking dish. Add enough boiling water to come halfway up sides of small dishes.

3 Bake puddings 20 minutes, whisking gently with fork under the skin of the puddings twice (this stops the rice from sinking to the bottom of the dishes). Sprinkle puddings with cinnamon; bake further 20 minutes, or until set. Let puddings stand 10 minutes before serving.

prep + cook time 1 hour **makes** 6

nutritional count per pudding 19.7 g total fat (13.4 g saturated fat); 366 cal; 37.2 g carbohydrate; 9.1 g protein; 2.3 g fiber

tip You will need to cook ⅓-cup white medium-grain rice for this recipe.

storage Puddings can be stored, covered, in the refrigerator for up to 2 days.

lemon tarts

This recipe is gluten-free, wheat-free, yeast-free, and nut-free.

. . . .

1 Process flours, superfine sugar, and butter until crumbly; add enough of the water to make ingredients come together. Knead dough gently on floured surface until smooth.

2 Preheat oven to 350°F/325°F convection. Grease six 4-in-deep removable-bottom tart pans.

3 Divide pastry into six portions. Roll one portion at a time between sheets of parchment paper until large enough to line pans. Ease pastry into pans, pressing into base and side; trim edges, prick base with fork. Cover; refrigerate 30 minutes.

4 Place pans on baking sheet; cover pastry with parchment paper, fill with dried beans or uncooked rice. Bake 10 minutes; remove paper and beans carefully from pastry shells. Bake further 10 minutes; cool.

5 Reduce oven temperature to 325°F/300°F convection.

6 Make **lemon filling**; whisk mascarpone and eggs together in large bowl until smooth. Add sifted sugar, rind, and juice; whisk until smooth. Divide filling among pastry liners.

7 Bake tarts about 30 minutes, or until the surface is firm to touch. Remove from oven; cool. Refrigerate 2 hours before serving, dusted with sifted confectioner's sugar.

prep + cook time 1 hour 15 minutes (+ standing and refrigeration)
makes 6
nutritional count per tart 45.4 g total fat (28.4 g saturated fat); 728 cal; 68.6 g carbohydrate; 11 g protein; 1.5 g fiber
storage Tarts can be stored in an airtight container in the refrigerator for up to 2 days.

1¼ cups rice flour
¼ cup cornstarch
¼ cup soy flour
⅓ cup superfine sugar
11 tablespoons cold butter, coarsely chopped
¼ cup cold water, approximately

lemon filling

1 cup (8 ozs) mascarpone cheese
4 large eggs
½ cup confectioner's sugar
1 tablespoon finely grated lemon rind
½ cup lemon juice

1 tablespoon confectioner's sugar

banana bread

This recipe is gluten-free, wheat-free, yeast-free, dairy-free, and egg-free.

2 tablespoons desiccated
  coconut
1½ cups mashed overripe
  banana
1¼ cups firmly packed light
  brown sugar
½ cup vegetable oil
2 teaspoons gluten-free
  baking powder
1 teaspoon pie spice
2½ cups desiccated coconut,
  extra
1¾ cups linseed, sunflower,
  and almond meal

1 Preheat oven to 350°F/325°F convection. Grease a 4 x 8-in loaf pan; coat base and sides with desiccated coconut. Shake out excess coconut.

2 Combine banana, sugar, oil, baking powder, and spice in large bowl, stir in extra coconut and meal. Spread mixture into pan; smooth surface.

3 Bake bread about 55 minutes. Let stand in pan 10 minutes; turn, top-side up, onto parchment-paper-covered wire rack to cool.

prep + cook time 1 hour 10 minutes (+ cooling) **makes** 10 slices
nutritional count per slice 34.3 g total fat (16.2 g saturated fat); 507 cal; 41.4 g carbohydrate; 7.4 g protein; 5 g fiber

tips You will need 3 large overripe bananas for this recipe.
This banana bread is good sliced and toasted.

storage Banana bread can be stored in an airtight container in the refrigerator for up to 1 week.

note Linseed, sunflower, and almond meal is a mixture of pulverized seed and almonds. It can be found in health-food stores or can be made by processing flax and sunflower seeds and almonds until finely ground.

passionfruit & lime crème brûlée

This recipe is gluten-free, wheat-free, yeast-free, dairy-free, and nut-free.

1 Preheat oven to 350°F/325°F convection.

2 Combine passionfruit, egg, egg yolks, sugar, and rind in medium heatproof bowl.

3 Bring coconut cream and milk to the boil in small saucepan. Gradually whisk hot cream mixture into egg mixture. Place bowl over medium saucepan of simmering water; stir over heat about 10 minutes, or until custard thickens slightly.

4 Divide custard among four deep ½-cup heatproof dishes. Place dishes in medium baking dish; pour enough boiling water into baking dish to come halfway up sides of dishes. Bake about 40 minutes, or until custard is set. Remove custards from water; cool. Cover; refrigerate 3 hours or overnight.

5 Preheat broiler.

6 Place custards in shallow flameproof dish filled with ice cubes. Sprinkle each custard with 1 teaspoon brown sugar; using finger, gently smooth sugar over the surface of each custard. Place dish under broiler until sugar caramelizes.

prep + cook time 1 hour (+ cooling and refrigeration) **serves** 4
nutritional count per serving 19.4 g total fat (14.1 g saturated fat); 269 cal; 16.6 g carbohydrate; 5.9 g protein; 3.5 g fiber

¼ cup passionfruit pulp

1 large egg

2 large egg yolks

2 tablespoons superfine sugar

1 teaspoon finely grated lime rind

1 (9-oz) can coconut cream

½ cup gluten-free soy milk

1 tablespoon light brown sugar

potato scones

This recipe is gluten-free, wheat-free, yeast-free, and nut-free.

1 stick butter, softened

⅓ cup confectioner's sugar

2 large egg yolks

1 cup cold mashed sieved
  cooked potato

2 cups gluten-free
  self-rising flour

2 teaspoons gluten-free
  baking powder

2 teaspoons milk,
  approximately

¼ cup raspberry jam

¼ cup heavy cream

1 Preheat oven to 425°F/400°F convection. Grease baking sheet.

2 Beat butter, sifted sugar, and egg yolks in small bowl with electric mixer until light and fluffy. Transfer to large bowl; stir in mashed potato.

3 Stir in sifted flour and baking powder; mix to a soft dough. Knead dough lightly on floured surface until smooth.

4 Press dough out to an even 1-in thickness. Dip a 2-in-round cutter into flour; cut as many rounds as possible from the dough. Place scones 1½ inches apart on tray. Gently knead scraps of dough together; repeat process.

5 Brush tops of scones with milk; bake about 25 minutes, or until scones sound hollow when tapped firmly on the top. Serve with jam and cream.

prep + cook time 40 minutes **makes** 12

nutritional count per scone 11.5 g total fat (7.2 g saturated fat); 175 cal; 31.5 g carbohydrate; 1.6 g protein; 0.8 g fiber

tip You will need to cook 1 large potato for this recipe.

storage Scones are best made and eaten on the same day. They can be frozen for up to 3 months. Thaw in oven, wrapped in foil.

chocolate cupcakes

This recipe is gluten-free, wheat-free, and yeast-free.

. . . .

1 Preheat oven to 300°F/275°F convection. Line a 12-hole (⅓-cup) muffin tin with paper liners.

2 Stir spread, chocolate, milk, and sugar in medium saucepan over low heat until smooth. Transfer to large bowl; cool 10 minutes. Whisk in sifted flours and cocoa powder until smooth. Divide mixture among paper liners.

3 Bake cupcakes about 35 minutes. Let stand in pan 10 minutes; turn, top-side up, onto wire rack to cool.

4 Meanwhile, make **fudge frosting**. Stir superfine sugar, spread, and the water in small saucepan over low heat until sugar dissolves. Combine sifted confectioner's sugar and cocoa in small bowl; gradually stir in hot sugar mixture until smooth. Cover; refrigerate 20 minutes. Beat frosting until spreadable. Transfer to pastry bag.

5 Using a ¾-in star tip, pipe fudge frosting onto cooled cupcakes.

prep + cook time 1 hour 10 minutes (+ cooling and refrigeration)
makes 12
nutritional count per cupcake 14.9 g total fat (3.8 g saturated fat); 309 cal; 49.4 g carbohydrate; 1.6 g protein; 0.6 g fiber
storage Cupcakes can be stored in an airtight container in the refrigerator for up to 3 days.

4 ozs dairy-free spread

3 ozs bittersweet chocolate (70% cocoa solids), coarsely chopped

¾ cup gluten-free soy milk

¾ cup superfine sugar

1 cup gluten-free self-rising flour

½ cup gluten-free all-purpose flour

2 tablespoons cocoa powder

fudge frosting

¼ cup superfine sugar

2 ozs dairy-free spread

2 tablespoons water

¾ cup confectioner's sugar

2 tablespoons cocoa powder

sticky date cakes with orange caramel sauce

This recipe is gluten-free, wheat-free, yeast-free, and dairy-free.

1 cup pitted dried dates

¾ cup boiling water

1 teaspoon baking soda

4 ozs dairy-free spread

¾ cup firmly packed light
  brown sugar

4 large eggs

2 cups almond flour

½ cup desiccated coconut

½ cup rice flour

orange caramel sauce

2 ozs dairy-free spread

½ cup firmly packed light
  brown sugar

⅓ cup orange juice

1 Preheat oven to 350°F/325°F convection. Grease two 6-hole jumbo (¾-cup) muffin tins; line base of each pan hole with parchment paper.

2 Combine dates, the water, and baking soda in bowl of food processor. Place lid in position; let stand 5 minutes. Process until almost smooth.

3 Meanwhile, beat spread and sugar in small bowl with electric mixer until light and fluffy. Beat in eggs, one at a time (mixture will curdle). Transfer to large bowl; stir in almond flour, coconut, and sifted flour, then the date mixture. Divide mixture among pan holes.

4 Bake cakes about 25 minutes. Let stand in pan 5 minutes before serving.

5 Make **orange caramel sauce**. Melt spread in small frying pan. Add sugar; stir over heat until dissolved. Add juice; cook, stirring, until sauce thickens slightly.

6 Serve warm cakes with hot orange caramel sauce.

prep + cook time 50 minutes **makes** 12

nutritional count per cake 23.5 g total fat (4.7 g saturated fat); 400 cal; 38.5 g carbohydrate; 7.3 g protein; 3.6 g fiber

tip You can substitute the almond flour for hazelnut or pecan flour if you prefer.

storage The orange caramel sauce is best served immediately once prepared because it will separate on standing.

brazil nut bread

This recipe is gluten-free, wheat-free, yeast-free, and dairy-free.

· ·

1 Preheat oven to 350°F/325°F convection. Grease a 4 x 13-in rectangular tart pan and line with parchment paper.

2 Beat egg whites in small bowl with electric mixer until soft peaks form. Gradually add sugar, one tablespoon at a time, beating until sugar dissolves between additions.

3 Transfer mixture to medium bowl; fold in sifted flour and rind, then nuts. Spread into pan.

4 Bake bread about 30 minutes; cool in pan. Wrap bread in foil; refrigerate 3 hours or overnight.

5 Preheat oven to 300°F/275°F convection.

6 Using serrated knife, cut bread into ⅛-in slices; place slices in a single layer on parchment-paper-lined baking sheets. Bake about 15 minutes, or until crisp.

prep + cook time 1 hour (+ refrigeration and cooling) **makes** 48 slices

nutritional count per slice 2.3 g total fat (0.5 g saturated fat); 35 cal; 2.9 g carbohydrate; 0.7 g protein; 0.3 g fiber

storage Brazil nut bread can be stored in an airtight container for up to 1 week.

2 large egg whites
⅓ cup superfine sugar
½ cup gluten-free
   all-purpose flour
1 teaspoon finely grated
   orange rind
1 cup brazil nuts

christmas pudding

This recipe is gluten-free, wheat-free, yeast-free, dairy-free, and egg-free.

2 cups golden raisins

1½ cups coarsely chopped
raisins

1 cup coarsely chopped
pitted dried dates

1 cup coarsely chopped
dried figs

½ cup slivered almonds

1½ cups water

1 cup firmly packed light
brown sugar

7 ozs dairy-free spread

½ cup brandy

2 tablespoons golden syrup
(available at specialty food
shops and some supermarkets)

1 cup soy flour

1 cup rice flour

2 teaspoons pie spice

1 teaspoon cream of tartar

½ teaspoon baking soda

1 cup almond flour

1 Stir fruit, nuts, the water, sugar, spread, brandy, and golden syrup in large saucepan over low heat until spread melts. Transfer mixture to large heatproof bowl; cool.

2 Grease a 9-cup pudding steamer; line base with baking paper.

3 Stir sifted dry ingredients and almond flour into fruit mixture. Spoon mixture into steamer, cover pudding with greased foil; secure with lid or kitchen string.

4 Place steamer in large saucepan with enough boiling water to come halfway up side of steamer; simmer, covered, about 6 hours, replenishing water as necessary to maintain level. Let stand in steamer 10 minutes before inverting pudding onto a platter.

prep + cook time 6 hours 15 minutes **serves** 12

nutritional count per serving 23.9 g total fat (3.2 g saturated fat); 627 cal; 83.5 g carbohydrate; 9.8 g protein; 8.2 g fiber

tips Chop all fruit a similar size to the raisins. Use orange juice instead of brandy, if you like. Cut holly leaves from lightweight card; bend gently to shape.

storage Pudding can be stored, covered, in the refrigerator for up to 1 month.

fruit cakes

This recipe is gluten-free, wheat-free, yeast-free, dairy-free, and nut-free.

. . . .

1 Line six 3½-in-round cake pans with two thicknesses of parchment paper, extending paper 2 inches above side.

2 Stir raisins, currants, peel, chopped pineapple, spread, sugar, brandy, and the water in medium saucepan over medium heat until spread is melted and sugar is dissolved; bring to the boil. Remove from heat; transfer to large heatproof bowl. Cool.

3 Preheat oven to 300°F/275°F convection.

4 Stir eggs into fruit mixture then sifted dry ingredients. Divide mixture among pans; decorate with cherries and pineapple wedges.

5 Bake cakes about 1 hour 10 minutes. Cover hot cakes with foil; cool in pans overnight.

prep + cook time 1 hour 30 minutes (+ cooling) **makes** 6

nutritional count per cake 31.4 g total fat (5.9 g saturated fat); 948 cal; 141 g carbohydrate; 13.1 g protein; 7 g fiber

tip When buying candied (also called glacé) fruit check the ingredients label for signs of "glucose made from wheat'" – glacé fruit is available without glucose, making it gluten-free and wheat-free.

storage Cakes can be stored in an airtight container in the refrigerator for up to 1 month.

1½ cups golden raisins

1 cup raisins,
    coarsely chopped

1 cup dried currants

2 tablespoons finely chopped
    candied citrus peel

⅓ cup coarsely chopped
    candied pineapple

7 ozs dairy-free spread

¾ cup firmly packed light
    brown sugar

⅓ cup brandy

⅓ cup water

3 large eggs

¾ cup rice flour

¾ cup soy flour

3 teaspoons gluten-free
    baking powder

1 teaspoon ground cinnamon

1 teaspoon ground nutmeg

½ teaspoon ground clove

18 green candied cherries, halved

3 slices candied pineapple,
    cut into wedges

orange shortbread

This recipe is gluten-free, wheat-free, yeast-free, egg-free, and nut-free.

2 sticks butter, softened
3 teaspoons finely grated
  orange rind
½ cup superfine sugar
1¾ cups gluten-free
  all-purpose flour
⅓ cup rice flour
1 tablespoon granulated sugar

1 Preheat oven to 300°F/275°F convection. Grease two baking sheets.

2 Beat butter, rind, and superfine sugar in small bowl with electric mixer until light and fluffy. Transfer mixture to large bowl; stir in sifted flours in two batches. Knead dough lightly on floured surface until smooth.

3 Divide dough in half; shape each, on separate trays, into 8-in rounds. Score each round into twelve wedges; prick with fork. Pinch edges of rounds with fingers; sprinkle the granulated sugar over them.

4 Bake shortbread about 40 minutes. Let stand 5 minutes; then, using sharp knife, cut shortbread into wedges. Cool on trays.

prep + cook time 1 hour (+ cooling) **makes** 24

nutritional count per shortbread 8.6 g total fat (5.6 g saturated fat); 145 cal; 16.3 g carbohydrate; 0.4 g protein; 0.2 g fiber

tip Try substituting the lemon rind for the orange rind and add ⅓-cup coarsely chopped dried cranberries to the dough.

storage Shortbread can be stored in an airtight container for up to 1 week.

fruit mince tarts

This recipe is gluten-free, wheat-free, yeast-free, egg-free and nut-free.

. . . .

1 Make **pastry**. Process flours, sugar, and butter until fine. Add enough of the water to make ingredients come together. Cover; refrigerate 30 minutes.

2 Combine fruit, brandy, the water, brown sugar, and spice in small saucepan; stir over low heat until sugar dissolves. Bring to the boil. Reduce heat; simmer, stirring, until liquid is absorbed and fruit is plump and tender. Stir in rind; cool. Blend or process cool fruit mixture until mixture forms a paste.

3 Preheat oven to 400°F/375°F convection. Grease a 12-hole jumbo muffin tin.

4 Roll pastry between sheets of parchment paper until ¼-in thick; cut 12 x 3-in rounds from pastry. Ease pastry rounds into pan holes, press into base and side; prick bases with fork. Spoon fruit mixture into pastry liners. Cut six 2-in stars; top six tarts with stars. Cut six 2½-in rounds from remaining pastry; cut 1-in stars from each round, discard these stars. Place rounds on remaining six tarts. Brush tops with a little extra water. Sprinkle tarts with superfine sugar.

5 Bake tarts about 15 minutes. Serve dusted with sifted confectioner's sugar.

prep + cook time 50 minutes (+ refrigeration and cooling) **makes** 12
nutritional count per tart 11.2 g total fat (6.9 g saturated fat); 308 cal; 43 g carbohydrate; 2.6 g protein; 1.7 g fiber
storage Tarts can be stored in an airtight container for up to 3 days. Fruit mince mixture will keep in an airtight container in the refrigerator for up to 1 month.

½ cup coarsely chopped raisins
½ cup golden raisins
⅓ cup dried cranberries
⅓ cup finely chopped dried apple
½ cup brandy
¼ cup water
2 tablespoons light brown sugar
1 teaspoon pie spice
1 teaspoon finely grated lemon rind

pastry
1¼ cups rice flour
¼ cup cornstarch
¼ cup soy flour
⅓ cup superfine sugar
11 tablespoons cold butter, chopped
2 tablespoons cold water, approximately

1 teaspoon superfine sugar
2 teaspoons confectioner's sugar

strawberry meringue cakes

This recipe is gluten-free, wheat-free, and yeast-free.

. . . .

14 tablespoons butter,
   softened
2¼ cups gluten-free
   self-rising flour
1 cup superfine sugar
½ cup milk
2 large eggs
2 large egg whites
½ cup strawberry jam
3 large egg whites, extra
¾ cup superfine sugar, extra

1 Preheat oven to 375°F/350°F convection. Line two 12-hole (⅓-cup) muffin tins with paper liners.

2 Beat butter in medium bowl with electric mixer until light and fluffy. Sift flour and ¼-cup of the superfine sugar together; beat flour mixture and milk into butter, in two batches, just until combined.

3 Beat eggs and egg whites in small bowl with electric mixer until thick and creamy. Gradually add remaining sugar, one tablespoon at a time, beating until sugar dissolves between additions. Gradually beat egg mixture into flour mixture just until combined.

4 Divide mixture among paper liners; bake cakes about 20 minutes. Transfer, top-side up, to wire rack to cool.

5 Increase oven temperature to 425°F/400°F convection.

6 Cut deep 1-in-wide hole from center of each cake; discard cake tops. Fill holes with jam.

7 Beat extra egg whites in small bowl with electric mixer until soft peaks form. Gradually add extra sugar, one tablespoon at a time, beating until sugar dissolves between additions. Spoon meringue mixture into large piping bag fitted with ½-in plain tip. Place cakes on baking sheets; pipe meringue on top of each cake. Bake 5 minutes, or until meringue is browned lightly.

prep + cook time 40 minutes (+ cooling) **makes** 24
nutritional count per cake 7.6 g total fat (4.8 g saturated fat); 168 cal; 31.7 g carbohydrate; 1.7 g protein; 0.3 g fiber

tip For a dairy-free version of this cake, substitute dairy-free spread for the butter and soy milk for the milk.

storage Cakes can be stored in an airtight container for up to 2 days. Unfilled cakes can be frozen for up to 3 months.

glossary

almonds

sliced paper-thin slices.

flour almonds ground to a coarse flour texture.

slivered small pieces cut lengthwise.

arrowroot a starch made from the rhizome of a Central American plant, used mostly as a thickener.

baking powder a rising agent; consists of two parts cream of tartar to one part baking soda. Gluten-free baking powder is made without cereals.

brazil nuts a triangular-shelled oily nut with an unusually tender white flesh and a mild, rich flavour.

butter use salted or unsalted (sweet); 125 g is equal to one stick (4 ounces) butter.

buttermilk is commercially made like yogurt; sold alongside dairy products in supermarkets.

candied fruit (cherries, pineapple) when buying candied fruit check the ingredients label for "glucose made from wheat" – it is available without glucose, making it gluten-free and wheat-free.

candied ginger fresh ginger root preserved in sugar syrup.

cheese

cream a soft cow's-milk cheese with a fat content of at least 33%. Sold at supermarkets in bulk and packaged.

feta Greek in origin; a crumbly goat- or sheep's-milk cheese with a sharp, salty taste.

mascarpone an Italian fresh cultured-cream product made like yogurt. Whiteish to creamy yellow with a buttery-rich texture. Soft, creamy, and spreadable.

parmesan a hard, grainy cow-milk cheese.

pizza a commercial blend of varying proportions of grated mozzarella, cheddar, and parmesan.

ricotta a sweet, moist, soft, white, cow's-milk cheese; has a slightly grainy texture.

chicken tenderloins thin strip under the breast.

chocolate

bittersweet (70% cocoa solids) also called semi-sweet; made of a high percentage of cocoa liquor and cocoa butter, and little added sugar. We use bittersweet chocolate unless stated otherwise.

candy melts small discs of compounded milk, white or dark chocolate, ideal for melting and molding.

white contains no cocoa solids, deriving its sweetness from cocoa butter. Very sensitive to heat.

cinnamon dried inner bark of the shoots of the cinnamon tree; comes in sticks (quills) and ground.

cloves dried flower buds of a tropical tree; can be used whole or ground. They have a strong scent and taste so should be used sparingly.

cocoa powder also called unsweetened cocoa.

coconut

cream obtained commercially from the first pressing of the coconut flesh alone, without added water; the second pressing is sold as coconut milk. Available in cans and cartons from supermarkets.

desiccated concentrated, dried, unsweetened, and finely shredded coconut flesh.

flaked dried wide strips of coconut flesh.

shredded unsweetened thin strips of dried coconut.

coriander, fresh also called cilantro; bright-green-leafed herb with a pungent flavor.

cornflakes, gluten-free available from health food stores or the health-food section in supermarkets.

cornstarch also called cornflour; used as a thickener. Available made from corn or wheat.

cream of tartar acid ingredient in baking powder; used in confectionery mixtures to help prevent sugar from crystallizing.

cream we use fresh heavy cream (pure cream).
heavy a whipping cream with at least 35% fat content.
sour thick, commercially-cultured sour cream with at least 35% fat content.
cumin also called zeera or comino; has a spicy, nutty flavor. Available in seed, dried, and ground form.
currants dried tiny, almost black raisins named from the grape type native to Corinth, Greece.
dates fruit of the date palm tree, eaten fresh or dried. About 1½ to 2 ins in length, oval and plump; honey-sweet in flavor with a sticky texture.
dill used fresh or dried, as seeds or ground. Its feathery, frond-like fresh leaves are grassier and more subtle than the dried version or the seeds. Has an anise/celery sweetness.
dried cranberries dried sweetened cranberries.
eggs if a recipe calls for raw or barely cooked eggs, exercise caution if there is a salmonella problem in your area.
flour
all-purpose flour made from wheat. Also available gluten-free from most supermarkets.
bread mix, gluten-free a commercial gluten-free bread mix available from most supermarkets.
buckwheat not a true cereal, but flour is made from its seeds. Available from health-food stores.
chickpea also called besan or gram; made from ground chickpeas so gluten-free and high in protein. Available from health-food stores and the health-food section in most supermarkets.
potato made from cooked potatoes that have been dried and ground.
rice very fine, almost powdery, gluten-free flour; made from ground white rice.

self-rising all-purpose flour mixed with baking powder in the proportion of 1 cup flour to 2 teaspoons baking powder. Also available gluten-free from most supermarkets.
soy flour made from ground soy beans.
food coloring vegetable-based substance available in liquid, paste, or gel form.
garam masala literally meaning blended spices; based on varying proportions of cardamom, cinnamon, cloves, coriander, fennel, and cumin, roasted and ground together.
gelatin we use powdered gelatin. It is also available in sheet form known as leaf gelatin.
golden syrup a by-product of refined sugarcane available in some speciality food shops and some supermarkets.
hazelnut flour hazelnuts ground to a coarse meal.
linseed flour ground linseed (flax seeds). Available from health food stores and in the health-food section at some supermarkets.
linseed, sunflower, and almond meal (LSA) available from health food stores and in the health-food section at some supermarkets.
macadamias a rich, buttery nut. Has a high oil content so should be stored in the refrigerator.
mandarin also called tangerine; a small, loose-skinned, easy-to-peel, sweet, and juicy citrus fruit. Mandarin juice is available in the refrigerated section in most supermarkets.
milk we use whole milk.
sweetened condensed a canned milk product; milk with more than half its water content removed and sugar added to the milk that remains.
noodles, rice vermicelli also called sen mee, mei fun, or bee hoon; used in spring rolls and salads.

Before using, soak dried noodles in hot water until softened, boil briefly then rinse with hot water.

nutmeg the dried nut of a tree native to Indonesia; available ground or you can grate your own.

oil

cooking spray we use cholesterol-free canola oil.

hazelnut a mono-unsaturated oil, extracted from crushed hazelnuts.

macadamia pressed from ground macadamias. Available in some supermarkets and delicatessens.

vegetable oils from plant rather than animal fats.

onion

green also called scallion or (incorrectly) shallot; an immature onion picked before the bulb has formed, having a long, bright-green edible stalk.

red also called spanish, red spanish, or bermuda onion; a sweet-flavored, large, purple-red onion.

pancetta an Italian unsmoked bacon; pork belly cured in salt and spices then rolled into a sausage shape and dried for several weeks.

pecans golden brown, buttery, rich nut; walnuts are a good substitute. Also available in pieces.

pie spice a blend of ground spices usually consisting of cinnamon, allspice, and nutmeg.

pistachios green, delicately flavored nuts inside hard off-white shells. Available salted or unsalted in their shells; you can buy them shelled.

polenta also called cornmeal; a flour-like cereal made of corn (maize). Also the dish made from it.

poppy seeds small, dried, bluish-grey seeds; crunchy and nutty. Available whole or ground from delicatessens and most supermarkets.

pure maple syrup distilled from the sap of maple trees. Maple-flavored syrup or pancake syrup is not an adequate substitute for the real thing.

rice flakes, gluten-free available from the health-food section in most supermarkets.

rice, rolled flattened rice grain rolled into flakes; looks similar to rolled oats.

spinach also called english spinach. Baby spinach leaves are best eaten raw in salads; the larger leaves can be cooked, but only until barely wilted.

sugar

brown an extremely soft, finely granulated sugar retaining molasses for its color and flavor.

confectioners' also known as pure icing sugar or powdered sugar.

superfine also called caster or finely granulated table sugar. The fine crystals dissolve easily.

white a coarse, granulated table sugar, also called crystal sugar.

turmeric also called kamin; a rhizome related to galangal and ginger. Must be grated or pounded to release its pungent flavor. Fresh turmeric can be substituted with the more common dried powder.

vanilla

bean dried, long, thin pod from a tropical golden orchid; the minuscule black seeds inside the bean are used to impart a luscious vanilla flavor.

extract obtained from vanilla beans infused in water; a non-alcoholic version of essence.

watercress a peppery salad green; highly perishable, use as soon as possible after purchase.

yogurt we use plain whole milk yogurt unless stated otherwise.

zucchini member of the summer squash family.

conversion chart

measures

All cup and spoon measurements are level. The most accurate way of measuring dry ingredients is to use a spoon to fill the measuring cup, without packing or scooping with the cup, and leveling off the top with a straight edge.

When measuring liquids, use a clear glass or plastic liquid measuring cup with markings on the side.

Unless otherwise indicated, always work with room temperature ingredients. Cold liquids added to butter can cause any batters and icings to break. We use large eggs averaging 2 ounces each.

dry measures

IMPERIAL	METRIC
½ oz	15 g
1 oz	30 g
2 oz	60 g
3 oz	90 g
4 oz (¼ lb)	125 g
5 oz	155 g
6 oz	185 g
7 oz	220 g
8 oz (½ lb)	250 g
9 oz	280 g
10 oz	315 g
11 oz	345 g
12 oz (¾ lb)	375 g
13 oz	410 g
14 oz	440 g
15 oz	470 g
16 oz (1 lb)	500 g
24 oz (1½ lb)	750 g
32 oz	(2lb) 1 kg

liquid measures

IMPERIAL	METRIC
1 fluid oz	30 ml
2 fluid oz	60 ml
3 fluid oz	100 ml
4 fluid oz	125 ml
5 fluid oz (¼ pint)	150 ml
6 fluid oz	190 ml
8 fluid oz	250 ml
10 fluid oz (½ pint)	300 ml
16 fluid oz	500 ml
20 fluid oz (1 pint)	600 ml
1¾ pints	1,000 ml (1 litre)

length measures

IMPERIAL	METRIC
⅛ in	3 mm
¼ in	6 mm
½ in	1 cm
¾ in	2 cm
1 in	2.5 cm
2 in	5 cm
2½ in	6 cm
3 in	8 cm
4 in	10 cm
5 in	13 cm
6 in	15 cm
7 in	18 cm
8 in	20 cm
9 in	23 cm
10 in	25 cm
11 in	28 cm
12 in (1 ft)	30 cm

oven temperatures

These oven temperatures are only a guide for conventional ovens. For convection ovens, check the manufacturer's manual.

	°F (FAHRENHEIT)	°C (CELSIUS)
Very slow	250	120
Slow	275-300	150
Moderately slow	325	160
Moderate	350-375	180
Moderately hot	400	200
Hot	425-450	220
Very hot	475	240

index

a

apple
    & pear crumble 70
    & ricotta fritters 16
    apple chocolate cake 82

b

bacon, egg & parmesan pies 40
banana
    bread 101
    hotcakes 20
beef lasagna 36
berry frangipane tarts 77
biscuits, sweet potato 85
blueberry bubble bark 53
brazil nut bread 110
bread
    banana 101
    brazil nut 110
brownies, chocolate fudge 81
buttercake 62

c

cake(s)
    chocolate apple 82
    fruit 114
    lime & coconut 94
    mandarin, macadamia &
      polenta 66
    moist flourless chocolate nut 57
    passionfruit & white
      chocolate gelatin 61
    sticky date cakes with orange
      caramel sauce 109
    strawberry meringue 121
cakes, rice noodle 24

carrot cupcakes 58
cheese & pancetta muffins 39
cheesecake, raspberry 74
chicken fingers, crunchy 49
chocolate pecan cookies 73
chocolate nut cake, moist flourless
    57
chocolate
    & fruit crackles 54
    chocolate apple cake 82
    chocolate cupcakes 106
    chocolate strawberry tart 89
    fudge brownies 81
    ganache 57
    icing 82
    moist flourless chocolate nut
      cake 57
christmas pudding 113
coconut & lime cakes 94
coconut custard tarts 90
coconut rice puddings 97
cookies, chocolate pecan 73
corn & chive muffins, mini 50
crackles, chocolate & fruit 54
crème brûlée, passionfruit
    & lime 102
crumble, apple & pear 70
crunchy chicken fingers 49
cupcakes
    carrot 58
    chocolate 106
custard tarts, coconut 90

d

date cakes, sticky, with orange
    caramel sauce 109

e

egg, bacon & parmesan pies 40

f

florentines, orange & ginger 69
flourless chocolate nut cake,
    moist 57
frangipane tarts, berry 77
fritters
    apple & ricotta 16
    indian vegetable 32
frosting
    cream cheese 58
    fluffy 62
    fudge 106
fruit & chocolate crackles 54
fruit cakes 114
fruit mince tarts 118

g

ganache
    chocolate 57
    white chocolate 61
ginger and orange florentines 69
granola, toasted 15

h

hotcakes, banana 20

i

icing
    chocolate 82
    mandarin 66
indian vegetable fritters 32

j

jaffa pudding, self-saucing 93

l

lasagna, beef 36
lemon tarts 98
lime
    & coconut cakes 94
    & passionfruit crème brûlée 102
    curd meringue tarts 86

m

macadamia, mandarin &
    polenta cakes 66
mandarin, macadamia &
    polenta cakes 66
meat pies, mini 45
meringue
    lime curd meringue tarts 86
    strawberry meringue cakes 121
mini corn & chive muffins 50
mini meat pies 45
mini pizza squares 46
moist flourless chocolate nut cake
    57
muffins
    mini corn & chive 50
    pancetta & cheese 39

o

omelette wrap 28
orange
    & ginger florentines 69
    shortbread 117
orange caramel sauce, sticky
    date cakes with 109

p

pancetta & cheese muffins 39
passionfruit
    & lime crème brûlée 102
    & white chocolate gelatin cake
    61
    kisses 78
pastry 40, 45, 118
pear & apple crumble 70
pecan chocolate cookies 73
pies
    egg, bacon & parmesan 40
    mini meat 45
pinwheels, pizza 31
pizza
    mini pizza squares 46
    pinwheels 31
    potato & oregano 35
polenta
    mandarin, macadamia and
        polenta cakes 66
    zucchini, olive and tomato
        polenta fingers 27
porridge, rolled rice 19
potato & oregano pizza 35
potato scones 105
pudding
    christmas 113
    coconut rice 97
    self-saucing jaffa 93

r

raspberry cheesecake 74
rice noodle cakes 24
rice puddings, coconut 97
ricotta & apple fritters 16

rolled rice porridge 19

s

scones, potato 105
self-saucing jaffa pudding 93
shortbread, orange 117
sticky date cakes with orange
    caramel sauce 109
strawberry meringue cakes 121
sweet potato biscuits 85

t

tart(s)
    berry frangipane 77
    chocolate strawberry 89
    coconut custard 90
    fruit mince 118
    lemon 98
    lime curd meringue 86
toasted granola 15

v

vegetable fritters, indian 32

w

waffles with maple syrup 12
white chocolate &
    passionfruit gelatin cake 61
wrap, omelette 28

z

zucchini, olive & tomato
    polenta fingers 27

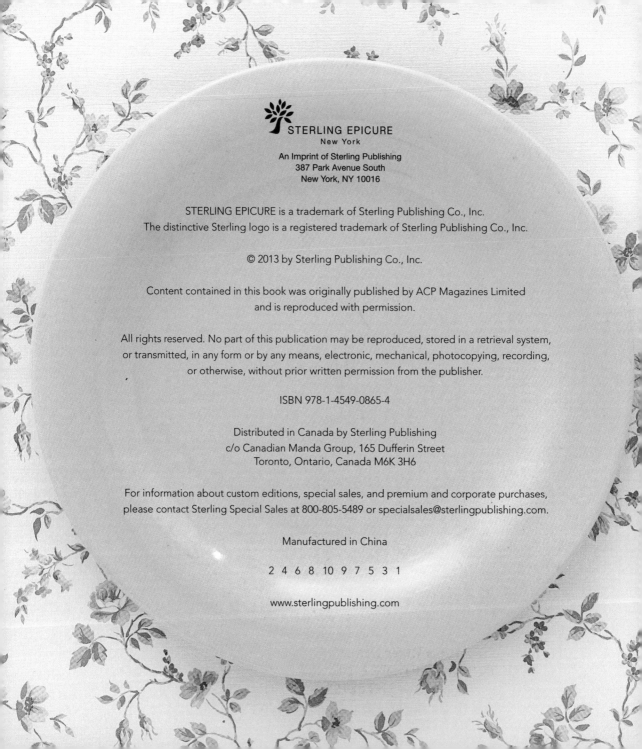

STERLING EPICURE
New York

An Imprint of Sterling Publishing
387 Park Avenue South
New York, NY 10016

ISBN 978-1-4549-0865-4

Distributed in Canada by Sterling Publishing
c/o Canadian Manda Group, 165 Dufferin Street
Toronto, Ontario, Canada M6K 3H6

For information about custom editions, special sales, and premium and corporate purchases,
please contact Sterling Special Sales at 800-805-5489 or specialsales@sterlingpublishing.com.

Manufactured in China

2 4 6 8 10 9 7 5 3 1

www.sterlingpublishing.com